NOT ART

a taxonomy

by **RYAN MULDOWNEY**
and **JACOB MULDOWNEY**

BRAZEN FLEECE PRESS

Published by Brazen Fleece Press
Copyright © 2018 by Ryan Muldowney and Jacob Muldowney

All rights reserved. No part of this publication may be reproduced, stored in a retrieval system, or transmitted in any form or by any means, electronic, mechanical, photocopying, recording, or otherwise, without written permission of the publisher, except in the case of brief quotations embodied in critical articles and reviews.

First Edition: October 2018

Printed in the U.S.A.

Summary: A taxonomic treatment of human endeavor that is primarily concerned with identifying what isn't art, in the hope of better understanding what is.

ISBN: 1726094367
ISBN-13: 978-1726094368
BISAC: Art / Criticism & Theory

The text type was set in Garamond.

For Ann and Chelsey

CONTENTS

Acknowledgments	i
Introduction	1
Chapter 1	9
Chapter 2	23
Chapter 3	31
Chapter 4	43
Chapter 5	51
Chapter 6	64
Chapter 7	73
Chapter 8	79
Chapter 9	87
Chapter 10	99
Taxonomic Diagram	107
About the Authors	109
Notes	111
Bibliography	118

ACKNOWLEDGMENTS

Our deepest gratitude to all those who read and edited various drafts of this text, and for all of the good advice we received, both solicited and unsolicited.

Further thanks are also due to the TCC ART 271 class, without whose recalcitrant positions on art this formalized argument would never have been conceived.

INTRODUCTION

Galileo once wrote, "[H]ow easy it is to understand ... all truths, once they are discovered; the point is in being able to discover them."[1] In so saying, Galileo suggests something about the nature of truth. Truth is not the fruit of some wayside tree to be casually harvested by every passerby. Truth is instead something that lies hidden.

If truth is hidden, our relationship to truth is consequently mitigated directly by our ability to uncover it and bring it to light. Discovery, therefore, is the coin of the realm to all those who wish to be acquainted with the truth. The pathway to discovery, however, is positively fraught with difficulties. Sometimes the price of discovery is the mastery of a complex process. Sometimes the price is the painstaking decoding of universal patterns, laws, and principles. Sometimes the price is the exhausting rigor of proofs, trials, and tests. In any event, unearthing even a kernel of lucid truth requires a great deal of exertion because truth is like a rare bird that inhabits the screes of a remote and precipitous crag. It is effectively invisible to all who are not looking, and for those who are, it can only be accessed through immense labor.

An additional burden of every discovery is the potential for having to alter long-held assumptions once a new truth is revealed. There is an obligation associated with the discovery of a truth, the obligation to assimilate that truth into one's life and ideology. This is typically less difficult for the individual who has already invested everything in the discovery of a truth, but for those that are not similarly invested, encountering newly discovered truth can induce a painful period of adjustment.

Galileo, who was no stranger to this phenomenon, wrote that "it is very unpleasant and annoying to see men, who claim to be peers of anyone in a certain field of study, take for granted certain conclusions which later are quickly and easily shown by another to be false ... [but have a] ... strong desire to maintain old errors, rather than accept newly discovered truths."[2]

It is not difficult to apprehend why this is so. Altering one's perspective to accommodate new truths as they emerge requires an admission that one's former views were incorrect, at least in part. The sheer discomfort of this kind of self-evaluation often prompts the formation of arguments designed to undermine inconvenient truths. To wit, there were many Ptolemaic adherents with ready arguments against the radical notion that the earth revolved around the sun for no better reason than because it was easier to disagree than it was to embrace a totally new worldview. To this point, Johann Wolfgang von Goethe said, "It is easier to perceive error than to find truth, for the former lies on the surface and is easily seen, while the latter lies in the depth, where few are willing to search for it."[3] This tendency toward facile skepticism is a strong temptation, as it allows for the indefinite deferral of a troublesome personal inventory.

The hidden nature of truth can understandably be very discouraging. More discouraging still is the fact that, for whatever reason, human limitations disallow for the perception of truth in its entirety: we are constantly discovering glimpses at the fringes of truth, but its totality as yet eludes us. This unfortunate reality, combined with the difficulty of approaching truth in the first place, seemingly provides ample justification for propping up such notions as "situational truth" and "personal truth". These, however, are merely quick fixes to the truth problem. What is more, the logical fallacies inherent to these ideas lead still others to wonder if there is such a thing as truth at all.

The sheer scale of the truth, and the manifest impossibility of mastering it all, should not be a bar to our belief in truth, and it shouldn't hinder our pursuit of it either. When considering the immensity of the cosmos, for example, it is evident that humans are unthinkably small. Nevertheless, in the face of this knowledge, mankind has consistently reached out, as far as his trivial capacities have allowed, in an effort to peer ever deeper into the mysteries of the universe. No astronomer would abandon the study of outer space simply because the whole picture was, ultimately, beyond their reach. In like manner, any pursuit of truth, whatever form it takes, is optimistically centered on the limitless potential for discovery, in spite of limited resources and capabilities.

To that end, imagine a great mountain, a fissured mountain larger than any continent, with many spurs and ridges running down to an infinite plain. Suppose you were to undertake the climbing of such a mountain. No matter where you began your ascent, the vast majority of a mountain of that scale would escape your view, and for such a mountain there would be no possible hope of descrying the ultimate pinnacle from the plain below. Truth is like this kind of a mountain, and anyone that would be acquainted with truth is required to climb.

In undertaking such a monumental climb, with no end in sight, it becomes difficult to know the nature and significance of any progress that is being made. While it is easy to see why these circumstances would lead some to abandon the ascent altogether, it is important to note that the inability to survey the whole of the mountain does not diminish the worth of what *can* be seen. Furthermore, it would be unreasonable to suggest that the inability to chart your progress relative to the whole topography of the mountain is an indication that no progress is being made. Even in making seemingly insubstantial progress up the mountain's rolling foothills you are still climbing the mountain, and by so doing you are elevating your gaze.

One might wonder if there is any value to this sort of progress if it never finds its ultimate conclusion. Consider for a moment the enormous wealth of this world. There is more money than any individual could possibly possess or spend. We do not scoff at the idea of money when we realize that we cannot possess all of it, nor do we round our shoulders in despair and just give up on money because we will only ever possess it in part. We are each severally content to own a portion of the world's total wealth, and remain undiscouraged by the fact that we will never own everything.

The possession of all truth may be similarly out of our reach, but we benefit all the same to the extent to which we are able to lay hold on any part of it. As our opportunities are increased in proportion with our access to the truth, we are clearly profited by acquiring as much truth as we are able to, regardless of whether or not we will ever possess it all.

There are innumerable avenues from which to begin an investigation of truth. There is truth to be found in agriculture just as there is truth to be found in architecture. Each of these avenues is like a spur of the aforementioned great mountain. While these disparate enterprises engender altogether different revelations about truth, they both remain connected to the more comprehensive fabric of ultimate truth. Philosophers and cabinet makers may seem to us to be climbing over very different terrain, but what appears at a distance to be independent parts of the mountain are inextricably connected the higher you climb. The seeming divisions that we see between these pursuits are merely a problem of perspective.

The reasons for choosing where on the mountain to make one's initial ascent has little to do with the "right way" to climb the mountain. Many mountains that attract climbers have scores of different routes that lead to the summit, and yet climbers will all have their favorites. One climber might prefer a particular route because it runs along tiers of waterfalls, while another might rather hike a different trail because it passes through thickly wooded slopes. Still another might choose to climb a path that stretches over meadows of alpine wildflowers. In most cases, what makes one path better than another to a climber has merely to do with the conditions of the intermediate stages of the climb rather than the ultimate destination.

Like philosophy and cabinet making, art is yet another track leading up the mountain of truth. Among so many potential points of entry, art is far from being the principal thoroughfare to truth, but there are nevertheless mountaineers that prefer to tread its paths because of the singular view. This is not to say that art is in and of itself truth, but that it forms a causeway that leads to ever-greater prospects of truth. To illustrate this idea, Pablo Picasso said, "We all know that Art is not truth. Art is a lie that makes us realize truth."[4] Picasso felt strongly that the truth to be found in art is not the art itself, but that which we come to understand through the process of viewing or making art.

The philosopher Herbert Marcuse expressed a similar idea when he said; "The truth of art lies in its power to break the monopoly of established reality ... to define what is real. In this rupture, which is the achievement of aesthetic form, the fictitious world of art appears as true reality."⁵ According to Marcuse, actual reality—being beyond the reach of the reality governed by our senses—is somehow made accessible to us through art.

The author George Sand echoed these sentiments further when she wrote, "Art is not a study of positive reality, it is the seeking for ideal truth."⁶ There is perhaps no better way to describe the nature of the great mountain than a reservoir of "ideal truth." Immeasurably large, universal, and stable, ideal truth is the bedrock of existence, and from these statements it seems clear that the primary function of art is to connect the artist and the viewer to that ideal truth.

Characterizing art thus—as an access point for truth—might seem to some as a bit overblown. After all, artists are often looked upon as eccentrics who produce somewhat trivial and superficial oddities of no great significance or societal value. Some might cynically observe that even if some few artists might enjoy a certain celebrity, their laurels come in consequence of the mounting auction prices commanded by their work rather than its revelatory power. These, and other similar views, do not appreciate the full measure of what art is ultimately meant to do.

If art can ever be used as a touchstone for truth, it must be properly understood. What it is and what it isn't suddenly become very important issues if we wish to lay eyes upon the revelatory vistas specific to its trails. We recognize, with Galileo, that the great difficulty of truth is in knowing where to find it, and in this book we undertake the task of mapping a bit of the mountain so that those who would perceive the specific truths available through art do not get lost along the way.

CHAPTER 1

What is Art? This is a question that is asked often enough in academic circles and lecture halls, at gallery openings and museums, and in important scholarly works. It is a question that has perplexed everyone from the Greek philosophers of antiquity to the bemused patrons of a contemporary exhibit featuring invisible art. It is a question that has surfaced again and again across millennia, spanning every culture and clime, and yet even today, it maintains a captivating influence on the human imagination.

This fascination with the question of what art is persists for the reason that art is an avenue that can connect us to the truth. An individual's success or failure in using art as a conduit to truth is largely mitigated by how clearly they comprehend what art is and what it does. A physician would not have much success taking a patient's temperature if he were to attempt to do so using a stethoscope. Likewise, the distinctive functions and attributes of art render it more suitable for pursuing certain types of truth than others, or at least more suitable for pursuing truth in a certain way. Hence the importance of determining the nature of art: if the question of art goes unanswered, its revelatory potential is squandered.

On the surface it might seem to some that the question "What is art?" is easily answered. For example, one might suggest that the term "art" simply refers to things like paintings, drawings, and sculptures. This response would not necessarily be a wayward impulse because until relatively recently in the history of art much of what was considered to be art found itself in one of these categories. However, even a summary examination of art's collected corpus demonstrates that painting, drawing, and sculpture, while covering a lot of ground, are not extensive enough to include every method of art-making.

Furthermore, painting, drawing, sculpture, or any other of the expanding list of processes used by artists are just that—processes. The presumption that art is the ineluctable byproduct of any attempt to make use of an "art material" cannot be countenanced as true. Look at it this way: the piano is a tool that is used by musicians to create music; it is a medium. We do not presume that all notes sounded upon a piano are automatically music. A piano tuner plays every note of the keyboard in the course of his task, but he is not playing music. Young piano students run through exercises in scales, arpeggios, and chord progressions, but they are not playing music either. Scales, arpeggios, and chords are some of the components from which music *can* be created, but in and of themselves they do not constitute music. In like manner, every pencil set to paper is not automatically art. It therefore follows that art must necessarily be more than merely what it is made of or the method whereby it is made.

If art is not strictly a consequence of medium or technique, we might go on to think that maybe art is more probably defined as the product of an artist reproducing or reinterpreting what he sees. There is quite a lengthy tradition in this sort of thing. Portraits, figures, animals, still lifes, genre scenes, landscapes are all based on observable phenomena, and these subjects have interested artists for ages. In fact, there are so many extant works within these categories that it sometimes seems as if you will see little else in the great museums of the world.

Although there is certainly a long and well-documented history of representation in art, the emergence of nonobjective art in the 20th century shook these traditions to their core. Much of Modernism came into being as a direct response to the idea that the historical attachment to representing or duplicating an observable motif was an unnecessary stricture upon artists.

The Abstract Expressionists, for example, saw representation merely as a gimmick and not a prerequisite for the creation of art. Many even viewed the task of rendering or interpreting objects or scenes from the visible world as a misguided notion, something at odds with art's inherent properties and a hindrance to fully capitalizing on what it is that art does best.

It is not difficult to fathom this reasoning. If the acme of achievement in art were the ability to perfectly establish the illusion of realism, excellence in art would have a finite apogee. This ceiling would effectively create an artistic dead end, for if the perfect illusion of realism is the best an artist can hope for, once that level of illusionism is realized, the progress of the artist grinds to a halt. It follows, therefore, that art is not about representation or illusion or even interpretation. It is about something else altogether. As the art critic and theorist Clement Greenberg put it:

> The essence of Modernism lies, as I see it, in the use of characteristic methods of a discipline to criticize the discipline itself, not in order to subvert it but in order to entrench it more firmly in its area of competence ... It quickly emerged that the unique and proper area of competence of each art coincided with all that was unique in the nature of its medium.[7]

Modernism, and its radical departure from traditional realism, charged itself with proving that the revelatory nature of art remained quite intact even when artists were making works that were inward looking and wholly divorced from representation.

Clement Greenberg went on to say, "Realistic, naturalistic art had dissembled the medium, using art to conceal art; Modernism used art to call attention to art."[8] Greenberg argues that the illusion created by artists in naturalistically reproducing something seen in the observable world is *an* art that disguises *actual* art. In other words, the substance of art is larger and more important than simply the skill of the artist in accurately representing a subject. Modernism shattered the need for these illusions, and by the time Abstract Expressionism rolled around in the mid-20th century, not only was there no need for illusions, there was no need for an observable subject at all.

Nonobjective art is hardly the only exception to the notion that all art is the product of an artist reproducing what he sees. Most of the cultures of the world have at one point or another made use of stylization or non-naturalistic invention in the creation of their art. Ethnographic art such as African masks and totems, Pre-Columbian ceramics and stone carvings, and Indian textiles and reliefs are all wonderful examples of a cultural penchant for non-naturalistic stylization.

In Western art history, figures like Hieronymus Bosch, Francisco Goya, Marc Chagall and many others dreamed up in their paintings worlds that never were. In so doing they demonstrated a greater degree of devotion to their own imagination than they did to the duplication of the physical world.

When we take into account much of the realm of conceptual art, and just about all avant-garde art from the postmodern era to the present, there seems to be no end of exceptions to the idea that art is primarily about reproducing what is seen.

If art cannot, therefore, be entirely circumscribed by the idea of representing something physical, perhaps art can be more effectively understood as the representation of something emotional. Many have asserted that art is most simply described as a mechanism for self-expression. The capacity to express oneself is critical in finding belonging. Language, even among the erudite and eloquent, is often a painfully inadequate tool in expressing thoughts and feelings.

Is art, then, primarily a medium for communicating through emotion that which cannot be transmitted through language? Vincent van Gogh expressed as much when he said:

> What am I in the eyes of most people—a nonentity, an eccentric or an unpleasant person—somebody who has no position in society and never will have, in short, the lowest of the low.
>
> All right, then—even if that were absolutely true, then I should one day like to show by my work what such an eccentric, such a nobody, has in his heart.
>
> ... I want to get to the point where people say of my work: that man feels deeply, that man feels keenly. In spite of my so-called coarseness ... perhaps even because of it.[9]

Van Gogh admitted his personal idiosyncrasies had led people to dismiss him, but he also saw his art as the very thing that would help others to see past his disagreeable tangibles to who he really was, and to what was really in his heart. By all accounts, most of his contemporaries might never have supposed from his behavior that Vincent van Gogh was capable of sensitivity. Through his work, however, we are able to see with new eyes the depth and tenderness of his feelings, and we, thereby, discover newfound empathy for the man.

James Castle is another interesting case study of art as a means of self-expression. Castle was born profoundly deaf, was reputedly illiterate, and had little recourse to any viable mode of communication with anyone, including his parents with whom he lived. Notwithstanding these circumstances, he taught himself to draw by mixing soot from the hearth with his own spit. By applying this makeshift medium onto the backs of packaging paper, old bags, and cardboard scraps by means of improvised mark-making tools of his own design, he was able to produce a massive body of work.

The man lived in rural Idaho at the beginning of the 20th century. He knew nothing of the art world, nothing of museums or great collections of art, and nothing of art historical figures. His art was a genuine effort at creation within a vacuum. When we ponder the possible motives for this compulsive, almost rabid work ethic—knowing full well that he had no notions of fame or fortune as an artist—we are left to conclude that art was perhaps the most effective way for James Castle to express that which was, for him, not transmissible through language.

There is plenty of evidence that the personal expression of ideas or emotions has been a deeply important use of art across time, and it is difficult to overstate the impact of this particular artistic function. However, in order to posit that the emotional or even ideological self-expression of an artist is art's defining characteristic, then everything that can be considered as art must necessarily fall under that umbrella. A summary examination of art history indicates that this is not the case.

As a rule, self-expression comes from within. It is the act or process of summoning forth something from the hidden depths of your person and bringing it to light. For art to be expressive, it therefore follows that it must reflect something that is intrinsic to the artist, and a great deal of what is commonly considered to be art does not fit this description.

By way of illustration, most historical artwork created prior to the 19th century was created at the behest of art patrons. Commissioned work, by its very nature, is bound up hand and foot by the inclinations of the client, and represents the creation of art that does not necessarily express something intrinsic to the artist. What is reflected in commissioned work is often the expression of something extrinsic to the artist and intrinsic to the customer.

A good example of the expressive compromise that happens when working for patrons is the career of the artist Jacques-Louis David. David first painted for the monarchy of Louis XVI. He later joined up with the likes of Robespierre and the Jacobins during the French Revolution, painted pictures promoting the sanguinary cause of the revolutionaries, and then, when the Reign of Terror drew to a close with the rise of Napoleon Bonaparte, David happily promoted the new emperor and his conquests as well. Each of these entities for whom David worked were diametrically opposed to what the others stood for, and yet David worked for them all, contriving in one career to express all of their conflicting worldviews.

In his famous painting, *The Oath of the Horatii* David promotes the idea of self-sacrifice among the citizenry for love of the king, the sort of thing a monarch would like. His painting, *The Lictors Bring to Brutus the Bodies of His Sons*, refers to the preservation of the Republic by any means necessary, even the execution of traitorous family members. This he painted for the bloody-minded revolutionaries. For Napoleon he painted images like *Napoleon Crossing the Alps* that played to the vanity of the Emperor and identified him with other historical military geniuses like Hannibal and Charlemagne.

The career of Rococo painter Jean-Honoré Fragonard likewise provides an interesting example of art created on commission. His clients were the decadent elites of the French aristocracy, and the bulk of his work revolved around so-called poetical imagery: pictures of the gallantry of that age. In reality, the gallant pictures so loved by the French aristocracy were little more than flossy erotic scenes. They didn't make for great art, but more to the point, they didn't make for much in the way of expression either. Fragonard's work was encumbered by the circumstance of catering to other tastes than his own.

On occasions when Fragonard was offered a court commission, he was given very specific guidelines to follow. "This applies to The Swing painted in 1766 for Baron de Saint-Julien, who had given him precise instructions for the posing of each figure."[10] There could be no image more iconic of French Rococo painting than *The Swing*, and yet the very composition of that piece was meticulously prescribed by a member of the court to the point where Fragonard said of the Baron de Saint Julien that "he asked me to paint madame (pointing out to me his mistress) on a swing being pushed by a bishop. I was to place him in such a way that he could see the legs of this beautiful child, and even more."[11] We can see that not only was the subject matter under the control of the client, but specifics related to content and the formal arrangement of compositional details were dictated to the artist as well.

It is hard to view the work of David or Fragonard wholly as the product or expression of something uniquely internal. In both cases, their work was constantly beholden to external forces. All artists who work for patrons find themselves, to one extent or another, similarly curtailed in their capacity to be expressive. The entire enterprise is founded upon the shelving of a personal agenda in favor of the demands of a client.

Other corners of the art world that make the "all art is self-expression" idea problematic include photorealism, the aim of which is duplicative in nature, not expressive. Expressive marks would wholly undermine the principle objective of photorealism, and as a result, photorealists do everything in their power to eliminate the hand of the artist in order to manufacture their illusions.

Artists who make use of a workshop to create their work are also problematic to the conception of art as being principally self-expressive in nature. An example of this can be witnessed in the person and the practice of the artist Andy Warhol. Warhol famously ran an enormous workshop—aptly named *The Factory*—with clouds of assistants making his art for him. In one interview, when the artist was asked to speak to the meaning of a specific piece, Warhol was unable to provide any answer himself, and in turn had to ask one of his assistants what the piece was about in order to provide a response.[12] This demonstrates that not only was Warhol not closely involved in the physical creation of his own work, he wasn't even connected to the ideation and content that the work represented.

Based on the above examples, it would appear that categorizing art as a function of self-expression lacks universal application to many artworks already in existence, and it must therefore be rejected as an inadequate answer to the question "What is art?"

Another possible definition of art, espoused by many, is that "Art is anything creative." Many have posited this in the hope that by casting a large enough net they will be able to draw a neat line around art. Because all art is creative in nature, this definition appears at first glance to be airtight. Granting that all art is creative, can we make the reverse argument: i.e. that everything creative is art? Since in this definition of art, art is a subset of creativity, it cannot necessarily follow that all creativity is art, in much the same way that all squares are rectangles, but not all rectangles are squares.

There are many creative enterprises that we do not

readily associate with the creation of art. The surgeon's endeavor in developing new procedures is certainly a manifestation of creativity, but it is difficult to conceive of it as an artistic undertaking. Likewise, many cybercriminals are very creative in finding and exploiting network and system weakness, but that cannot really be considered art either. Furthermore, when your mechanic fixes your car's undercarriage with zip ties instead of ordering factory-made fasteners, his solution is the byproduct of creativity, but it is not art.

Clearly, casting too small a net is problematic in seeking to uncover the nature of art, but it is equally problematic to cast a net that is too large. Such is the case when making statements such as "Art is anything creative," or even broader statements such as "Everything can be art," or "Art is *in* everything," or worse still "Art *is* everything."

These arguments are troublesome because they prop art up as an unknowable, ineffable entity without boundaries, meaningful description, or purpose. There are some that seem to rejoice in the incomprehensible complexity implied by such an assertion, as if the incomprehensibility suggested by this argument were strong evidence of its truth. However, preaching the doctrine of incomprehensibility does not by default bolster the importance of a thing, and actually understanding a thing does not minimize its impact. Sometimes things are incomprehensible solely for the reason that they are either not well understood or well explained, or because they are utter nonsense.

If everything were art, regardless of intrinsic purpose, value, function, or meaning, then we are forced into some strange conclusions about art. "Everything" is comprised of an infinite number of objectives that largely find themselves at cross-purposes. If art were everything, it would be a good evil, a worthless treasure, a virtuous vice, a healthy sickness, and a meaningful meaninglessness. If everything is art, then art is wholly contradictory and simply stands for nothing. If art stands for nothing, then it has no conceivable worth, nor can it conceivably exist.

It seems clear that, by default, not everything is art, but Gertrude Stein gave us a glimpse into why many may believe art is everything when she said, "Art isn't everything. It's just about everything."[13] Because art is a thing that can potentially embark into every territory and make use of any or every thing as its subject, this understandably confuses many into believing everything is art. "Everything," however, is infinite in quality, quantity, and nature; art is not. Art has boundaries. Art has limitations. Ad Reinhardt said, "The one thing to say about art is that it is one thing. Art is art-as-art and everything else is everything else ... Art is not what is not art."[14] According to Reinhardt, art is divisible from everything else. The infinite is indivisible. If art is divisible from everything else it must be finite, and therefore not everything.

Thus far, in seeking to answer the question "What is art?" we have only been able to dredge up unsatisfactory non-conclusions. Perhaps the real difficulty in answering the question of art is not so much a product of our inability to formulate reasonable conclusions as it is the nature of the question itself. The real problem with the question "What is art?" is that the answer has to be extricated with almost surgical precision from everything else. This presents us with a complicated and even delicate endeavor since "everything" encompasses such an array of seemingly interconnected categories. Attempting to answer the question "What is art?" is further problematic because in order to prove or disprove whatever definition is arrived at requires that the definition be tested by comparison, in this case to everything, which is a time consuming proposition.

Instead of answering the question "What is art?" perhaps a better starting point would be to answer the question "What is *not* art?" In doing so, it may be possible to definitively dismiss a great number of undertakings as being unrelated to the field of art. By narrowing the scope of what can possibly be considered art, we find ourselves on a much more solid basis for later attempting to theorize about the true nature of art, for "When you have eliminated all which is impossible, then whatever remains, however improbable, must be the truth."[15] By systematically designating what art is *not*, we are more readily able to identify in the end what art actually *is*.

CHAPTER 2

As alluded to in Chapter One, at least part of the difficulty in coming to a useful conclusion about the nature of art stems from the tools that we allow ourselves to use in the creation of our artistic propositions. The overly orthodox preconceptions about art that we often cherish may actually limit our access to useful, alternative lines of reasoning and can become barriers to a full understanding of what art is. What if the question of art was approached from a different perspective? What if different kinds of arguments were admissible?

In prioritizing an understanding of what *isn't* art as the first step in understanding what *is* art, we step off a well-trodden but meandering track of established rhetoric and argumentation and find ourselves traversing relatively virgin soil. Our motivation in doing so does not stem simply from jejune contrariness; there is a real need to access theoretical tools elsewhere that are frankly unavailable in the typical deliberations about the nature of art. By allowing ourselves to look outside the conventional territory of art discourse and expanding the bandwidth of our conversation to include an appreciation of art in context, we are afforded access to additional repositories of evidence, patterns, and principles unavailable to those whose arguments about art look only inward.

To that end, if we are able to admit that at least a portion of art is concerned with approaching truth, it follows that we might glean some insights about art from analogous disciplines that are similarly engaged in the search for truth. Scientific inquiry, for instance, is fundamentally concerned with bringing truth to light. Physics, astronomy, geology, medicine, biology, chemistry and many other areas of scientific study directly involve themselves in drawing back the cosmic curtain in an effort to reveal new truths. They do so with the aid of many efficient instruments and methodologies.

If art and science are both involved in the search for truth, it is not incredible, therefore, that some of the strategies used by the sciences could be profitably applied in seeking to more accurately uncover the nature of art. Before embarking on a more scientific approach to the question of art's nature, however, it is necessary that we first dispel certain ideas about the relationship between artistic and scientific endeavor.

It is not uncommon, for example, to encounter the belief that art and science are almost wholly incompatible. This perception, however, is inaccurate, as it stems from clichés about both disciplines. Many believe that because of the emotional components of art, art must be irrational. It is also widely believed that because art is so closely bound up with individualism, it must therefore be subjective in nature. If art is irrational and subjective, many feel forced to conclude that anything said about art can have no real foundation in truth, and must therefore be erected upon the shifting sands of opinion.

Science, on the other hand, is widely viewed as being dispassionate, and because it is seen as emotionless and clinical we presume that it must be wholly rational. Since science deals in facts, it is perceived as entirely impartial and objective. Many conclude, therefore, that if science is rational and objective, dealing only in facts, then it is absolutely—even exclusively—reliable in cutting to the heart of the truth. These clichés shape the prevailing views of these two areas of inquiry, and as a result, it is not altogether surprising that art and science should so often be considered as irreconcilable.

These long entrenched stereotypes were dismissed by Albert Einstein when he said, "[A]rts and sciences are branches of the same tree. All these aspirations are directed toward ennobling man's life, lifting it from the sphere of mere physical existence and leading the individual towards freedom."[16]

That freedom to which Einstein referred is truth, and lest we think one branch of his proverbial tree superior to another in the article of truth, his associate Bertrand Russell observed that, "Science as the pursuit of truth is the equal, but not the superior, of art."[17] The perceived differences between science and art arise merely from the methods they employ to arrive at their mutual objective.

But upon comparison, even the methods employed by the two disciplines bear more than a passing resemblance to each other. Art, like science, revolves around principles, formulas, systems, and laws. The artist is concerned with the theories underlying the nature and behavior of light. The artist is a student of the laws that govern the properties of color and color interactions. The artist uses perspectival systems and formulae to understand and document spatial relationships. All of these very basic functions of art are profoundly connected to science.

Because most art relies upon sensorial cues, most art is a manifestation of empiricism. The senses form the tools that allow both the artist and the scientist to understand the nature of their subject. Observable data, and the interpretation of that observable data, is as fundamental to an artist as it is to a scientist.

Further comparisons between art and the sciences include mathematical concepts such as ratios, proportion, and geometry. The ancient Greeks, for example, were obsessed with notions of ideal aesthetic beauty, and they concluded that beauty—something that we now often consider to be subjective—was an objective study that had its basis in ideal mathematical constructs. For them, math provided the empirical proofs of ideal beauty, and accordingly, Greek artists subscribed to those principles in the creation of their art.

Specific examples of the use of mathematics in art

include, of course, the Greek sculptors Polykleitos and Lysippos, both of whom created proportional systems for mathematically understanding the ideal human figure based on a set of ratios. Later, no doubt inspired by these efforts, the Roman polymath Vitruvius also based his own work on the geometry of the human figure. During the 15th century, luminaries such as Brunelleschi, Masaccio, and Piero della Francesca were all considered true "renaissance men," that is, men of both science and art. Brunelleschi in particular is largely credited with having rediscovered the system of rules governing linear perspective, an innovation that was adopted as a central tenet of all artistic endeavor for centuries thereafter.

Even modernists had connections to math and science in the creation of their systems. Paul Cezanne, and the cubists that would follow him, were determined to, "treat nature by the cylinder, the sphere, the cone,"[18] and in the mid-20th century, the Bauhaus turned out a whole generation of artists obsessed with geometry and visual mathematical harmonies.

Additionally, an interest in anatomy—another scientific field—has been a core tenet of Western art since the time of the Greeks and the Romans. During the Italian Renaissance, artists made use of scientific methods such as dissection in an effort to understand the human form as profoundly as did their classical forebears. Tellingly, "In the second half of the sixteenth century officials in Florence authorized the release of cadavers for dissection not only to physicians (understandable, to modern minds) but also to artists,"[19] which would seem to put medicine and art on a roughly equivalent standing.

Moreover, anatomical scenes of dissection appear in the works of artists from Rembrandt to Thomas Eakins. Auguste Rodin was so skilled in his scientific understanding of skeletal, vascular, and muscular anatomy that he was accused of "surmoulage," or the casting of human figures instead of sculpting them.

The philosopher David Hume drew a line directly connecting the science of anatomy with art when he said, "The anatomist presents to the eye the most hideous and disagreeable objects, but his science is useful to the painter in delineating even a Venus or a Helen."[20]

The artist's curiosity about the natural world does not stop with the study of human anatomy. Countless artists have further developed interests in the scientific studies of biology, zoology, botany and mineralogy.

For instance, dating back to the 15th century, and long predating the Age of Enlightenment, the *Ghent Altarpiece* painted by Jan and Hubert van Eyck is littered with flowers, grasses, shrubs, trees, and bushes that are so detailed in their description that they are identifiable by modern scientists as specific botanical species. James Sowerby and John James Audubon were both naturalists for whom there was no incompatibility between art and science. Their drawings and paintings of plants, animals, and minerals illustrated their scientific exploits and materially advanced scientific knowledge and understanding about the natural world.

The study of the properties and interactions of the chemical world have also positioned artists alongside scientists. The discovery of chemical processes used in everything from the creation of frescoes and etchings, to the formulation of painting mediums and ceramic glazes, to the development of film and darkroom photography further denote shared ground between the artistic and scientific communities.

Furthermore, artists, like scientists, are inventors, and have for centuries been interested in contriving optical tools such as viewfinders, mirror systems, lenses, camera obscura, and other mechanical apparatuses to help them to see the world more clearly. These artistic advances are not far removed in nature or in practical function from the scientific development of the telescope, the microscope and the X-ray machine.

If more evidence were needed to argue the similarities that exist between science and art, we might also refer to the fact that whole movements of art have grown out of areas of scientific inquiry, such as pointillism, op art, metaphysical art, and surrealism. The preponderance of observable connections between these two fields of study make the contention that art is diametrically opposed to and wholly incompatible with science simply untenable. We must conclude, therefore, in spite of the prevailing views, that art and science are more alike in purpose, method, and function than not.

However, it is not only that art is more like science than we commonly recognize, but science in its turn is more like art than is usually believed. Using the term "poetry" to mean the highest achievement of the arts, the English philosopher Herbert Spencer said:

Let us not overlook the further great fact, that not only does science underlie sculpture, painting, music, poetry, but that science is itself poetic. The current opinion that science and poetry are opposed is a delusion. ... On the contrary science opens up realms of poetry where to the unscientific all is a blank. Those engaged in scientific researches constantly show us that they realize not less vividly, but more vividly, than others, the poetry of their subjects.[21]

Science and art ultimately draw water from the same well; there is no competition or antipathy between the two. Many may find this to be a revelation, in part because they have not understood science, but more probably because they have not understood art. Understanding that art is related to science is an important point of departure because it allows us to consider scientific analysis as a reasonable methodological approach to answering the question of art, and establishing that idea allows us to theorize about the nature of what art is—or is not—from a more objective, facts-based point of reference.

CHAPTER 3

If we can conclude that art and science are more closely related than is commonly supposed, it stands to reason that some of the tools that are used to evaluate and organize scientific concepts can be implemented to good effect in the pursuit of a more crystalline understanding of art. If our aim is to clarify the nature of art by first discovering what is unquestionably not art, then taxonomy—the branch of science concerned with classification—would appear to be an especially valuable scientific tool in such an enterprise.

Over the centuries, scientists have manufactured systems to help them to understand the nature of matter, cellular biology, anatomy, mineralogy, botany, zoology, and so forth. Carl Linnaeus, the architect of binomial nomenclature and the modern classification of the natural world said:

The first step in wisdom is to know the things themselves;

this notion consists in having a true idea of the objects; objects are distinguished and known by classifying them methodically and giving them appropriate names. Therefore, classification and name-giving will be the foundation of our science.[22]

For Linnaeus, the name by which a thing was called and the order to which it belonged was an essential characteristic of understanding the essence of the thing itself. In his own efforts to make sense of the natural world, Linnaeus made use of taxonomy for the systematic, hierarchical classification of all biological phenomena. Linnaeus divided everything up into kingdoms, classes, orders, etc., in an effort to understand the family relationships that exist within nature. By similarly making use of the science of classification to identify patterns within art, we may likewise be afforded fresh perspective about how the various branches of human endeavor are related—or more to the point, not related—to the field of art.

It is probable, however, that the idea of shoehorning art into some sort of a manufactured system is expressly repugnant to the poetical sensibilities of many individuals. There are certainly those who might feel that the enclosing of art into a set of parameters puts it on a leash and diminishes its capacity to surprise and to move us.

Perhaps there are those who believe that restricting art to its own little cubbyhole would drain away its mystery and establish it once and for all in the mundane province of formula. Since "formula" is a term generally used to describe things that are predictable, reproducible, and ultimately unoriginal, reducing art thus would be, for many, an effrontery, particularly since it is not uncommon for originality to be perceived as the gold standard for excellence in art. The conception that an insuperable compatibility problem exists between formula and originality is founded upon a fundamental misunderstanding of what the nature of originality is.

As C.S. Lewis once wrote:

> Even in literature and art, no man who bothers about originality will ever be original: whereas if you simply try to tell the truth (without caring twopence how often it has been told before) you will, nine times out of ten, become original without ever having noticed it.[23]

In short, the surest indication that originality will elude you is if originality is your primary pursuit. Even when achieved, originality is not necessarily a sufficient end unto itself, as is humorously illustrated by the composer and comedian Peter Schickele and his "doctrine of originality through incompetence."[24]

History is brimming with examples of creative individuals who managed to be original while nevertheless working within the constraints of convention and formula. 19th century author Jane Austen's romance novels were most decidedly written according to a formula, and yet they are almost universally heralded as masterpieces of literature. By all accounts, grinding the same grist again and again did no injury to her work. Johann Sebastian Bach's work was the stuff of conventional Baroque tastes, and yet he is considered widely to be one of the greatest composers of all time, and somehow head and shoulders superior to his contemporaries who were employing the same compositional formulas as he was. Rembrandt's predictable use of extreme light and dark in his paintings was likewise hardly original, but what original unoriginality! Rembrandt's work casts a long shadow over the world of painting to this day.

We may ask ourselves why the creativity and even originality of these individuals appears to have been undamaged by their working within fairly narrow parameters. A simple biological example might explain this idea in part. When human beings have a child, that child is composed of a finite palette of genetic material contributed by both the father and the mother. Each subsequent child that comes along is different, even though they are conceived by the same method, and arise from an identical gene pool. No matter how many children there might be in a family, they will all be different, including twins. In spite of the fact that the creation of families is in many respects the product of formulaic methods and materials, there is still seemingly endless space for variability and uniqueness within the confinement of that sphere.

Art is similarly capable of making infinitely nuanced, original works even when those works seem to be confined by highly restrictive criteria. For example, many artists have deliberately narrowed their focus to produce whole series of monochromatic paintings, that is, paintings that simply cover the canvas with a single color.

While at first blush it might seem that there could be no material difference between one entirely gray painting and another, a close examination of the separate pieces would likely demonstrate a host of distinct characteristics between them, including the body and surface of the paint, the rhythms and textural signatures left by the movement of the brush, to say nothing of potential disparities in scale, shape, and orientation.

Speaking of his own monochromatic paintings, the artist Gerhard Richter put it this way, "This is just a grey surface. Painted grey. It surprised me, too: when I started to make grey paintings my motivations weren't very serious ... But then I noticed differences in quality: they were all grey, but some were better."[25]

No two gray paintings are alike. Even when artists consciously impose restrictions upon themselves, they always seem to have plenty of space to move around in. We must conclude, therefore, that true originality stems, not merely from dramatically diverging from all known convention, but rather from the infinitely ingenious ways in which one works within a set of parameters.

Returning to the argument that systematic classification would limit art, we grant that this is necessarily true. However, it is not an unfortunate truth. As has already been demonstrated, "art without limitations" is useless. The value of art is directly connected to the way in which it responds to its own limitations. Being corralled within the loose box of classification in nowise diminishes art.

Further objections that could be raised with regard to the classification of art might revolve around the accuracy of such a system. Can everything that is art, or not art, truly be captured by a taxonomy, with nothing being left out or misplaced? Is it possible to keep everything that is not art from being co-mingled with art? If there were any exceptions to the classifications, would that not undermine the credibility of the entire structure?

These are all good questions. In answer, we need only refer back to the original scientific models that inspired this idea of a taxonomic analysis of art in the first place. All scientific systems have outliers, no matter how rigorously constructed. The platypus is a perfect example of this sort of thing. Under Linnaean classification, the platypus presents a problem. It has fur and nurses its young (mammalian traits), it has a bill (an avian attribute), and it is venomous (a characteristic most commonly connected to insects, reptiles and sea creatures). It is important to recognize that the platypus does not render the whole taxonomy invalid, rather, it creates the opportunity to fine tune the model further by adding fresh wrinkles of complexity to the larger whole, and thus refine the shape of revealed truth.

To this point, Georges-Louis Leclerc declared:

Nature progresses by unknown gradations and consequently does not submit to our absolute division when passing by imperceptible nuances, from one species to another and often from one genus to another. Inevitably there are a great number of equivocal species and in-between specimens that one does not know where to place and which throw our general systems into turmoil.[26]

But he goes on to say:

> In general, the more one augments the number of divisions of the productions of nature, the more one approaches the truth, since in nature only individuals exist, while genera, orders, and classes only exist in our imagination.[27]

While the manufacture of a system without any outliers is an improbability, it seems clear that the more information we add to a system of classification—the more relationships, divisions, and subdivisions we are able to reasonably make—the greater our chances of seeing a picture that resembles the truth. This understanding highlights the need for any discussion regarding the nature of art to avoid addressing art as an isolated entity. Rather, the conversation should be couched within a broader framework, which can be accomplished by investigating the surrounding terrain that provides the context for art.

Understanding how art is related to some things and unrelated to others is critical to appreciating its place and its impact in the world. As previously discussed, it is for this reason that arguments that consider art in isolation are largely unsatisfactory. Imagine if a biographer were to write the biography of an individual while only making use of that person's private journals as his source material. Approaching the writing of a biography in that manner would prove problematic for the reason that seeking to understand an individual solely from the perspective of his own self-perception paints a pretty one-dimensional picture.

In order to see the larger picture and understand the complexity of that individual, a biographer will typically draw on numerous sources that give context to his arguments. Letters and other accounts from friends and relatives create an invaluable layer of context in seeking to understand the subject, as does information provided by colleagues, supervisors, and even rivals of the individual. Historical details about contemporaneous linguistic, societal, cultural, religious, philosophical and political trends further help to widen the lens.

A biographer's efforts to reveal the true nature of an individual rely on seeing the subject as part of a larger fabric. Writing about a person without addressing the contextual modifiers of that individual's life would be something like trying to perform a violin concerto with just the soloist and no accompanying orchestra. Disassociated from the larger whole, the soloist could provide but a dim fragment of the broader score. It is the same when we talk about art while ignoring everything that surrounds it.

While understanding what separates "not art" from "art" might appear as something of a peripheral side show, it is actually fundamental in uncovering larger ideas about art, and a taxonomy is necessary to supply us with an adequate frame of reference for understanding what doesn't belong in the discussion of art and why.

One of the principle ways in which a taxonomy like that of Linnaeus attempts to establish truths is through the identification of observable patterns. Once a pattern is identified, it can then be used as the basis for theorization.

For example, birds come in all shapes and sizes, but certain specimens exhibit similar morphological patterns. One group of birds might have hooked beaks, broad, short wings, and sharp talons, while another group of birds might have long, narrow wings, webbed feet, grooved bills, and an underdeveloped hind toe. Within the Linnaean taxonomy, birds with similar physical characteristics are grouped together because a shared morphology implies shared behavior. It can be assumed that a bird with a webbed foot can swim, just as it can be assumed that a bird with a hooked beak and talons eats meat.

By taking note of observable patterns such as these, we can extrapolate reliable conclusions about the habits and economy of these creatures. Identifying and organizing observable patterns in nature is not the manifestation of a scientific compulsion to tidy up all of creation. A taxonomy is a hypothesis, and the development of a hypothesis is a core component of the scientific method.

Paleontologist Stephen Jay Gould expressed this idea eloquently when he said:

> Taxonomy (the science of classification) is often undervalued as a glorified form of filing—with each species in its folder, like a stamp in its prescribed place in an album; but taxonomy is a fundamental and dynamic science, dedicated to exploring the causes of relationships and similarities among organisms. Classifications are theories about the basis of natural order, not dull catalogues compiled only to avoid chaos.[28]

The organizational relationships within patterns are important, not only because of what can be apprehended about the things that make up the component parts of the pattern, but also because of what can be understood about how all of those components intermingle in the formation of a much larger whole.

Theoretical physicist Richard Feynman put it this way, "Nature uses only the longest threads to weave her patterns, so that each small piece of her fabric reveals the organization of the entire tapestry."[29] In other words, the pattern and what the pattern is made of are inextricably connected. You cannot see the nature of the one without simultaneously seeing something of the nature of the other.

Patterns reflect a stability that is closely associated with the fingerprints of truth, but patterns are not the same as truth. They merely point to the presence of truth, or at least the direction one must go to find it. Patterns are shaped by principles, laws, or rules. By identifying a pattern, we position ourselves to theorize about the rules that govern that pattern. Once we have credibly understood the rules of the pattern, we can point directly at unseen truth. Just think of the simple patterns that elementary school children are taught to assess.

Complete the next four steps of the following pattern:

1 , 3 , 5 , 7 , _____ , _____ , _____ , _____

As the above pattern is recognized, the following set of rules or principles from which the pattern arises is apprehended:

1. This pattern is made up of numbers only.
2. The numbers in this pattern must all be odd numbers.
3. Each subsequent number in the pattern is the same as the previous number plus 2.

An understanding of the rules or principles that brought the pattern into being allow the student to identify unseen truths (i.e. the next four steps in the pattern) and thereby accurately presuppose the ongoing nature of the pattern infinitely.

As a practical application of this kind of idea, modern baseball makes use of advanced statistics in an effort to win ball games. Analysts record reams of information about the patterns of play for every player in the league, and they are able to gather such comprehensive data from the historical patterns of individual player performance that they can predict a player's response to certain situations.

If it is known that Player A has never hit the ball to left field in 3,000 at bats and hits line drives or grounders 89% of the time he connects with the ball, we have identified a pattern. This pattern allows the defensive team to extrapolate the principles of Player A's performance, and this information in turn allows the defending team to shift the positioning of its fielders to increase their chances of successfully defending against Player A's statistically likely response to a pitch.

The statistically likely response is the unseen truth; it is what was theorized upon from the analysis of a pattern of play. The analysis of patterns leads to the unearthing of principles, and acting on principles leads to the discovery of hidden truths. There are likewise patterns in art that are founded upon principles, laws and rules. By making use of a taxonomic system of classification we are able to identify the patterns common to things that *are* art, and differentiate them from the patterns that exist among things that are *not* art.

CHAPTER 4

Thus far, we have laid some important groundwork in our approach to the question "What is art?" or perhaps more appropriately, "What is not art?" We have confirmed that art is a highly complex undertaking. We have also observed that at least a portion of the confusion that sometimes surrounds art arises from a general incapacity to describe with precision what art actually is and what art actually does. While we have demonstrated that it is a simple matter to draw up a definition of art that is either on the one hand too narrow, or on the other hand too broad, it is another thing altogether to develop a meticulous and exact description of the nature of art that allows for the smallest possible number of exceptions.

We have focused at length on the shared function of both art and science—that of bringing truth to light—and we have hypothesized that the assimilation of truth is either directly or indirectly the object of all art, all science, and ultimately every worthwhile human endeavor.

We have demonstrated that art is much more related to science and scientific methods than is widely understood. We have suggested the counterpoint as well, that science is somewhat more artistic than is commonly believed. These observations have led us to the conclusion that art and science, while admittedly different, are more analogous than is ordinarily supposed. Indeed, they are enough alike for us to reasonably benefit from the utilization of scientific tools in the refinement of our understanding of art.

To that point, we have recognized the scientific practice of classification as a potent tool for identifying and organizing observable patterns, and that by understanding the principles and laws responsible for the formation of these patterns we become empowered to theorize about the nature of unseen truths. We have determined that by submitting art to a taxonomic system of classification we can categorically establish where "art" resides within the context of a sea of things that are "not art."

Our first concern in doing so is to determine the best shape for our taxonomic structure. Like the Linnaean model, we want to organize all of our inputs by comparative breadth or significance. In other words, the broader or more significant a category, the higher order its function and the higher up it belongs in the taxonomy. Conversely, the smaller and more specific a category, the lower order its function and the further down it belongs. These systems are best read from the top down, so the real question is, where to start? What is the broadest topic to be appropriately included in our model?

Since our particular focus is not strictly concerned with evaluating art in isolation, but rather where art belongs within the spectrum of human endeavor, art will of necessity be at the very bottom of our taxonomy. This means that we will need to establish a "big picture" that can be divided and subdivided layer by layer until, finally, we arrive at art. If all art is a function of human endeavor, what is all human endeavor a function of? The answer, in a word, is "life," and since we are unaware of anything of a higher order than that, life must be where our taxonomy begins.

It becomes necessary to theorize about the purpose of the highest order function of our model so that all subsequent divisions align to address that purpose. What then, we might ask, is the purpose of life? There are many potential responses to this question, but the answer that is most related to our argument is one we have already discussed at great length, i.e. that the fundamental purpose of human existence is to draw nearer to truth. If "life" is at the top of our system, and the purpose of life is to approach truth, then it follows that the functional subdivisions of "life" have to do with the various methods whereby we undertake the search for truth.

There are three general ways through which we can come in contact with the truth.

The first way that truth can be approached is through *Instruction*. Aristotle believed that, "The educated differ from the uneducated as much as the living differ from the dead."[30] Education here refers to the process whereby a vessel that is full of truth pours its contents into a vessel that is empty. Instruction occurs when someone who knows truth—i.e. an authority—transmits knowledge directly to those who don't. As Plato concluded, "Those who don't know must learn from those who do."[31]

The second way that truth can be approached is through *Inspiration*. This kind of revelatory experience is what led Archimedes to cry "Eureka!" as he saw with new eyes the principle of buoyancy, and it is likewise what led Sir Isaac Newton, with the help of a falling apple, to subsequently theorize about the nature of gravity. Plato too had experience with this particular pathway to truth, and he describes the phenomenon as follows, "With a sudden flash there shines forth understanding about every problem, and an intelligence whose efforts reach the furthest limits of human powers."[32] He describes here something that most people have experienced in one form or another, that is, an inexplicable "Aha" moment that comes out of the blue, or even a metaphysical or spiritual experience that draws back the curtain and allows for greater insight or expanded perspective.

The third way to encounter truth is through *Agency*, and this happens when we take it upon ourselves to unearth and decode hidden truth on our own. The etymology of the word "agency" derives from the Latin word for "doing." An agent is a person or a thing that takes an active role, a person that actively "does."

The philosopher Arthur Schopenhauer suggested that personal agency was perhaps the most important avenue in the search for truth when he wrote:

> Those who have spent their lives in reading, and have drawn their wisdom from books, resemble men who have acquired precise information about a country from many descriptions of travel. They are able to give much information about things, but at bottom they have really no coherent, clear, and thorough knowledge of the nature of the country. On the other hand, those who have spent their lives in thinking are like men who have themselves been in that country. They alone really know what they are talking about; they have a consistent and coherent knowledge of things there and are truly at home in them.[33]

> Reading is a mere makeshift for original thinking. When we read, we allow another to guide our thoughts in leading strings. Moreover, many books merely serve to show how many false paths there are and how seriously we could go astray if we allowed ourselves to be guided by them. But whoever is guided by genius, in other words thinks for himself, thinks freely and of his own accord and thinks correctly; he has the compass for finding the right way. We should, therefore, read only when the source of our own ideas dries up, which will be the case often enough even with the best minds. On the other hand, to scare away our own original and powerful ideas in order to take up a book, is a sin against the Holy Ghost. We then resemble the man who runs away from free nature in order to look at a herbarium, or to contemplate a beautiful landscape in a copper engraving.[34]

While our access to truth in the first two scenarios—instruction and inspiration—is largely at the mercy of extrinsic forces, agency is entirely self-determinative. For that reason, although there is much to be said about both instruction and inspiration, our immediate concern has mainly to do with agency. Agency, by its very nature, has a greater capacity to uncover previously unknown truths than does instruction—which by its nature deals in truths that are already known by at least one person—or even, in some cases, inspiration. Furthermore, access to instruction or inspiration can potentially be throttled by personal circumstances, while agency provides universal access to truth, regardless of an individual's situation.

The universality of agency underscores its importance as a tool for seeking truth. Agency is essential to any kind of sustained existence. Survival, for example, is fundamentally rooted in the capacity to independently solve such problems as how to avoid starvation or dehydration, how to avoid injury, how to avoid illness or disease, how to avoid extreme heat or cold, or—if one or more of these problems becomes inevitable—how to best adapt to new conditions.

While these dilemmas are without a doubt of prime importance, and the province of all living things, the choices that confront humans specifically are not just limited to questions of survival.

Aristotle said, "The ultimate value of life depends upon awareness and the power of contemplation rather than upon mere survival."[35] The fruits of human awareness and contemplation are both the ability and the desire to solve problems that are not related to survival. For example, C.S. Lewis wrote, "Friendship is unnecessary, like philosophy, like art ... It has no survival value; rather it is one of those things that give value to survival."[36] In short, in their use of agency, humans are not merely absorbed with the perpetuation of their species; they are also deeply concerned with the quality of their existence. This propensity would seem to be self-evident from the human penchant for active involvement in questions related to curiosity, personal happiness, meaning, and above all, truth.

Whether we are aware of it or not, our entire lives are, without exception, worn away in the perpetual grind of agency, of independently choosing and doing. For example, we are constantly and intractably enmeshed in such trivial functions of agency as exemplified in the questions, "Should I wake up on time?" or "Should I go to work?" or "What am I going to do this weekend?" We are also presented with more pressing and complex questions like, "How can I fix this relationship?" or "How do I feed my children when I don't have any money?" or "What kind of person do I want to be?"

Every independent choice that we as humans make is a function of agency, and since agency exists as a means to uncover the truth, we conclude that actively doing and choosing those things that can acquaint us with truth is fundamental to the purpose of agency and, therefore fundamental to the purpose of life. While art is a byproduct of agency—of the independent choice to do and to act in the discovery of truth—not every decision arising from agency leads to the creation of art. For this reason, a further examination becomes necessary in order to determine if there is a taxonomic need to additionally partition the variable operations of agency.

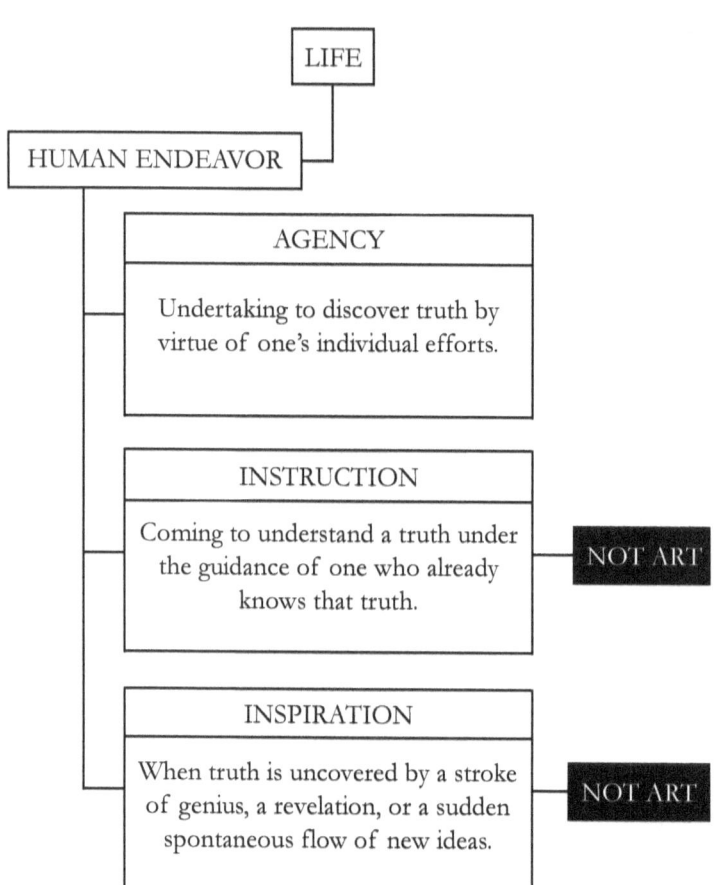

CHAPTER 5

As we have indicated, much of agency is engaged in what could reasonably be termed "problem-solving." In its most common usage, the word "problem" comes laden with certain baggage. Problems are typically viewed in a negative light and are seen as being synonymous with troublesome difficulty or hardship. While it is true that the province of agency is concerned with what choices to make when confronted with unpleasant situations or obstacles, the problem-solving aspects of agency are in reality much broader.

When we talk about a problem in mathematics, for instance, the term "problem" has no associated negative connotations, it merely means an equation to be figured out.

Similarly, a multiple-choice question on a chemistry test presents a different kind of problem. It does not necessarily follow that the problem in question is particularly troublesome or difficult. Rather, the problem in this instance is simply another kind of opportunity to exercise agency in choosing a response.

In that vein, and for the purposes of our taxonomy, every situation that demands action or reaction is essentially a problem to be solved. Therefore, as a function of agency, the term "problem-solving" refers to the whole bandwidth of what can be meant by the word problem: from trivial decisions in mundane situations, to the tackling of a full-blown existential crisis.

The use of agency to solve problems is central to the operation of society at nearly every level. Marketing firms solve the image problems of their clients. Food trucks solve lunch hour problems. Suppliers solve problems of production. Lawyers, sanitation workers, educators, bankers, retailers, lawn care professionals, and doctors are all in their own way engaged in solving some kind of problem.

Based on our understanding of what problem-solving entails, it becomes evident that the practice of creating art is also interested in the solution of problems. To be sure, art is frequently used as a medium to address problems inherent to other areas of inquiry—including politics, philosophy, communication, meaning, existential angst, aesthetics, or spirituality—but the creation of art can also be used as a way to explore and solve problems intrinsic to art itself. As Danish polymath Piet Hein observed, "Art is solving problems that cannot be formulated before they have been solved. The shaping of the question is part of the answer."[37]

The artist Chuck Close echoed this sentiment when he said:

> I think our whole society is much too problem-*solving* oriented. It is far more interesting to [participate in] "problem creation" ... You know, ask yourself an interesting enough question and your attempt to find a tailor-made solution to that question will push you to a place where, pretty soon, you'll find yourself all by your lonesome — which I think is a more interesting place to be.[38]

> ...[T]he most interesting thing is to back yourself into your own corner where no one else's answers will fit. You will somehow have to come up with your own personal solutions to this problem that you have set for yourself because no one else's answers are applicable.[39]

Art's capacity to be the creator of the very problems that it solves, and the resulting homespun discovery that this sort of activity lends itself to, creates a strong correlation between agency and art. The truth available to us through art comes most commonly from independent action, observation, and decision-making rather than from instruction. Art methods and practices may be taught, but how to open new doorways to truth must be discovered. While artists can know the influence of inspiration in their work, understanding in art typically comes from "doing." Artists do not wait idly for revelation to strike, they create opportunities to deliberately encounter that revelation.

While we might say that all art is an act of problem-solving, and therefore an act of seeking truth through agency (rather than through instruction or inspiration), it cannot reasonably be asserted that all attempts at discovering truth through agency—or even all acts of problem-solving—result in the creation of art. Certainly, it would require a truly singular worldview to make the claim that the aforementioned lawyers, sanitation workers, educators, bankers, retailers, and lawn care professionals—all of whom are clearly involved in solving some sort of problem—were also, in their respective roles, creating art. Since seeking truth through agency can be applied so broadly, to vastly different enterprises and for entirely disparate purposes, it becomes necessary for us to establish some further branches of our taxonomy in order to more precisely distinguish between art and everything else.

For our purposes, there are three ways that agency can be used to solve problems, and thereby approach truth.

The first way that agency can be employed to solve a problem is through *Procedure*. Solving problems through procedure can most easily be described as what results from an individual following a set of prepared instructions, a technique, or a formula. Assembling a piece of furniture by following the guidelines in a printed manual, for instance, is a function of procedure. There is a formulated assembly technique that follows a specific set of instructions in sequence to arrive at a predictable outcome, all of which are key elements of a procedural approach to solving a problem.

There are many kinds of everyday problems that are

routinely solved by procedure. Operating a vehicle, creating an email account, setting up a new mobile device, and even making toast are all functions of procedure. On a larger scale, manufacturers, publishing houses, food processing plants, and many other cornerstones of industry—whose brands and reputations are intrinsically linked to the uniformity of their product—require rigidly predictable outcomes in their problem-solving strategies. As a result, all of these enterprises, and many more like them, also make use of formula and technique—in other words, procedure—to ensure consistent outcomes.

Aside from assuring consistency, other advantages of procedural problem-solving can be found in the development of the modern bureaucracy. Each cog in the bureaucratic machine has its prescribed formulaic task. This separation of duties enables complex endeavors to be undertaken with a minimum of disruption. Max Weber describes the action of the ideal bureaucracy thus, "Precision, speed, unambiguity, knowledge of files, continuity, discretion, unity, strict subordination, reduction of friction and of material and personal costs - these are raised to the optimum point in the strictly bureaucratic administration."[40]

The second way that agency can be employed to solve a problem is through *Analysis*. Analysis differs from procedure in that its solutions arise in direct consequence of independent study or research, rather than a reliance on prescribed responses. While some measure of information is necessary as a basis for analysis, the process of analyzing lends itself to extrapolating from potentially limited data a more comprehensive understanding of a subject.

Consider the task of the archaeologist who, while excavating a site, encounters a cache of ancient artifacts. The mere discovery of the objects, while useful, provides little or no information on the culture from whence they stemmed. Without being subject to further analysis, the hypothetical artifacts would naturally generate more questions than answers. What are these objects? Who made them? Why were they made? What is their cultural significance? What is their historical value? What new information do these artifacts bring to light about the people who made them?

By comparing the artifacts with other known specimens, using radiocarbon dating techniques, and conducting chemical analyses of the materials, the archaeologist can confidently answer many of the aforementioned questions. Analysis can, in this way, lead to a whole swath of solutions that are beyond the reach of procedure.

There are many other fields that, like archaeology, are primarily focused on the collection, analysis, and interpretation of data. Geology, biology, botany, chemistry, astronomy, physics, and most other areas of scientific inquiry all rely on using a quantity of known information to draw conclusions about what is not known, and therefore hinge upon effective analysis. By that same standard, we can also conclude that mathematics, including arithmetic, calculus, algebra, trigonometry, and geometry are likewise analytical in nature.

The strength of analysis lies in its unbending capacity to meticulously dissect even seemingly inscrutable things in an effort to uncover the principles that govern the "how" and the "why" of those things. Because analysis is fundamentally connected to observable, measurable information, many important but nevertheless un-measurable intangibles fall outside of the scope of its competence.

The third way that agency can be employed to solve a problem is through *Creativity*. Unlike analysis, creative problem solving does not necessarily rely on observable information as a starting point for investigation. Speaking of the act of painting, the artist Andrew Wyeth highlighted the difference between analysis and creativity when he observed that, "If you clean it up, get analytical, all the subtle joy and emotion you felt in the first place goes flying out the window."[41] In other words, analysis, while effective in its own sphere, has the potential capacity to diminish or discard valuable truths like Wyeth's "subtle joy and emotion" simply because they reside outside the compass of analytical function.

Creativity is largely involved in the making of something completely new, the modification of something already made, or the manufacture of a novel interaction. Relying in general upon the imagination to envision a solution that as yet does not exist—sometimes, as already mentioned, to a problem that does not yet exist either—creativity is often involved in breaking new ground, and expanding the palette of potential solutions into unexplored territory.

Architects, fashion designers, city planners, and corporate strategists are all examples of creative problem solvers. Based on a specific set of situational requirements, these and other creative problem solvers have to literally imagine something into existence where there was nothing before.

To further clarify the difference between creativity versus analysis and procedure, consider the following scenarios. Someone who develops their own recipe is engaged in a creative act. Someone who merely follows that same recipe is involved in a procedural act. Someone who reverse engineers the correct recipe from an analysis of the dish would be involved in an analytical act. Though all three dishes would be materially the same, the act that brought them into being would not be.

While creativity, analysis, and procedure are three distinct functions of agency, it often happens that the solution to a given problem requires the simultaneous employment of a combination of the three. For example, if we were to imagine a large infrastructure project like a system of roads, bridges, or railways, it is easy to see how each of these problem-solving strategies would be required to realize the undertaking. The designers (functionaries of creativity) would conceive the vision for the project. They would imagine the look of the thing, its functionality, and how it would interact with the existing context. The engineers (functionaries of analysis) would analyze potential risks and make appropriate decisions about materials, safety, and structural requirements. They would also determine which sequence of processes would most efficiently bring the project into being. The contractors (functionaries of procedure) would execute the project based on a set of plans and instructions, making use of proven formulas, processes, and techniques.

This combination of problem-solving strategies, however, is not simply the domain of huge corporate endeavors that require the skills of large numbers of people. Sometimes, these strategies have to be used in combination by individuals working out complex problems on their own.

Consider the task of a medical doctor. A patient arrives at his office and describes a set of symptoms. Depending on the complexity of the symptoms, the doctor can deduce the source of the trouble. Often, further empirical tests are required to expand the scale of what is understood about the complaint. Blood tests, ultrasounds, X-rays, urine analysis, MRI's, and so forth all serve to widen the doctor's base of information. The more comprehensive the analysis of available data, the more likely a solution is to be found.

This diagnostic function of the doctor's profession is unquestionably analytical. However, once a diagnosis is determined, the doctor generally proceeds to administer prescribed treatments and healing techniques to effect a cure. These ministrations are not a function of analysis; they belong to the arena of procedure, inasmuch as they represent the employment of predetermined solutions to remedy specific maladies or problems.

In the event that the patient does not respond well to conventional treatments, the doctor will sometimes turn to unconventional or even experimental therapies in an effort to provide relief. These efforts are not procedural because they fall outside of the scope of tried and true solutions. Because the ordinary measures have failed, a new set of interactions is attempted upon in the hope of a desirable outcome. This kind of treatment is essentially a function of creativity. The work of a doctor, while primarily analytical in nature, is also procedural, but with the potential under certain circumstances to be creative as well.

What then can we conclude about things that are simultaneously creative, analytical, and procedural in nature? How do we classify them? Why is it even important to specifically classify something that is so potentially complex? Being able to specifically classify what area of agency a pursuit falls under is important for the reason that all art is primarily a function of creativity. If we are able to definitively determine what branch of agency an activity falls under, we can with confidence begin to make assertions about whether or not it is connected to art.

In cases where a combination of analysis, procedure, and/or creativity are used in concert, the key indicator for determining classification has mainly to do with the dominant problem-solving strategy in evidence. To illustrate how this would work, we will attempt to establish the dominant problem-solving strategy of something that can be used in a wide variety of situations, such as the medium of photography. Typically, it is assumed that, because so many artists have used photography as a medium, any photograph must therefore automatically be art. It is possible, however, since all art is a product of creativity, that if a photograph is not primarily creative in nature, it cannot be regarded as art.

Let us consider the case of a photo studio such as can be found in department stores or malls. The employees of these establishments are not hired for their creative genius, nor for their artistry; they are hired because they are able to follow a predetermined formula to create a predictable quality of photograph. They flip a switch to turn on pre-arranged lighting, they scroll to a preselected backdrop, and they push the shutter release on a camera that was set up specifically for optimal results in this particular setting. Given the nature of the process, it is easy to see that the photographs produced in this scenario are not creative, nor analytical, but are unmistakably procedure dominant.

Alternatively, consider a crime-scene photographer. As part of a team of forensic investigators, this kind of photographer is responsible for the analysis of a crime scene. This requires them to evaluate and photograph all of the particulars of a crime scene and its surroundings, including even small, seemingly insignificant details that might potentially prove critical to the investigation. There is nothing creative about this kind of documentary photography. Furthermore, since crime scenes vary considerably from one to the next, there is no strict formula or procedure that could be followed in photographing a given crime scene. While the end result of crime scene photography is the production of photographs, just like in the department store photo studio, the photographs produced in this case are clearly analysis dominant, not procedural or creative.

As mentioned above, art is primarily a product of creativity. The only type of photography that could possibly be countenanced as art is photography that is primarily creative. Because the photographs from the photo studio were principally a product of procedure, not creativity, we would not consider them to be art. Similarly, because the photographs of the crime scene photographer were analysis dominant instead of creativity dominant, we likewise cannot consider them to be art.

This same reasoning applies to determining the art potential of any given thing. Any venture that finds itself *primarily* under the aegis of procedure or analysis is not art. Changing the oil in your car is primarily procedural and is therefore not art. Fixing a washing machine is primarily analytical or procedural and is therefore not art. Diagnosing leukemia is primarily analytical and is therefore not art.

If all problem-solving endeavors are to be classified based on the dominant problem-solving strategy they employ, and all art is primarily a function of creativity, we are able to establish our first theory about "not art."

"Anything that is not primarily a function of creativity is not art."

NOT ART

```
┌─────────┐
│ AGENCY  │
└────┬────┘
     │
     ├──┬─────────────────────────────────┐
     │  │          CREATIVITY             │
     │  ├─────────────────────────────────┤
     │  │ Solving problems by making some-│
     │  │ thing new, modifying something  │
     │  │ that already exists, formulating│
     │  │ a novel interaction, etc.       │
     │  └─────────────────────────────────┘
     │
     ├──┬─────────────────────────────────┐
     │  │           ANALYSIS              │──── **NOT ART**
     │  ├─────────────────────────────────┤
     │  │ Solving problems through the    │
     │  │ analysis of existing information│
     │  │ in order to extrapolate that    │
     │  │ which is not yet known or       │
     │  │ understood.                     │
     │  └─────────────────────────────────┘
     │
     └──┬─────────────────────────────────┐
        │           PROCEDURE             │──── **NOT ART**
        ├─────────────────────────────────┤
        │ Solving problems by making use  │
        │ of established formulas,        │
        │ techniques and procedures.      │
        └─────────────────────────────────┘
```

CHAPTER 6

If all art can be shepherded into the fold of creativity, then creativity becomes our primary area of interest as we further continue to flesh out this particular branch of the taxonomy of human endeavor. But as all creativity is not alike, creativity itself is subject to further division. The most useful distinction to be made between different areas of creativity can be summed up in the differences that exist between *Organic Creativity* and *Design*.

Design is perhaps best described as deliberately manufactured creativity. As an outgrowth of problem-solving, design is the considered development and orchestration of a plan for the solution of a problem. Design is an infinitely various avenue of creativity that is commonly connected to systematic, formal constructs, principles, and rules, but it is not limited by them. Design is purposeful, it is forward-looking, it is methodical, it is rational, and above all, it is a premeditated act. Design does not happen by accident.

Organic creativity on the other hand is the kind of creativity that is reactive, impulsive, and more than anything else, improvised. It is the primitive creativity largely undertaken by those in a state of nature. We see examples of this kind of creativity repeatedly in the animal kingdom. Under the influence of an instinctual response to their context, the bird builds its nest, the beaver its dam, the termite its mound, the prairie dog its colony, and the bee its hive. These endeavors are without question creative in nature, but they are the byproduct of an irrational creativity, and are most often the result of a reactionary response to a particular "in the moment" need, making use of whatever materials happenstance has deposited close at hand.

Humans are as prone to organic creativity as any creature in the animal kingdom. When bothered by a wobbly table at a restaurant, one might fold up a paper napkin into a wad and stuff it into the gap under the shortest leg. When we suddenly need to prop open a door that is not equipped with a doorstop, we might use any heavy object that is on hand like a cinder block, or a box, or a trashcan in order to keep the door from swinging shut. When we need to hang a picture but do not have a convenient hammer, we might find something else with which to drive the nail, such as a rolling pin or a paperweight. All of these responses are primitive, impulsive, almost desperate solutions to an immediate problem. In every case, the solution does not rely upon a formal set of principles or systems.

Architect, designer, and theorist Buckminster Fuller

observed the distinction between acts of desperate creativity and design when he said:

> I am enthusiastic over humanity's extraordinary and sometimes very timely ingenuity. If you are in a shipwreck and all the boats are gone, a piano top buoyant enough to keep you afloat that comes along makes a fortuitous life preserver. But this is not to say that the best way to design a life preserver is in the form of a piano top. I think that we are clinging to a great many piano tops in accepting yesterday's fortuitous contrivings as constituting the only means for solving a given problem.[42]

The "fortuitous contrivings" mentioned here by Fuller are the products of organic creativity, and because these solutions arise instantaneously and are unconsidered, they are generally not as efficient as the products of design.

In some cases, the products of organic creativity and the products of design can appear deceptively similar. As an example of this, we might consider the way that towns and villages often came into being centuries ago. At the outset, a farmer or a herdsman might build his house close to cropland and grazing, a miller might build his house by the water to make use of the current, a mason might build his house on the hillside to have easy access to stone, a carpenter might build near a forest, and a shopkeeper would probably build in whatever spot was most conveniently located to all the rest.

Over the course of time, connecting footpaths might be established between the homes of the various inhabitants through the sheer action of individuals repeatedly taking the most direct or convenient course from house to house. With population increases, more and more footpaths connecting individuals and enterprises would no doubt arise. Later, some of these footpaths would turn into roads for wagons, carriages, and pedestrians, and new businesses would pop up along these public thoroughfares in an effort to profit from the concentrated volume of traffic. By and by, what was once a loosely connected congregation of organically formed footpaths would become the irrationally tangled network of a city.

In contrast, consider the city that is laid down according to principles of design. This kind of city is deliberately planned from the outset. Considerations such as the number of people the city will serve, what public amenities will be needed, and how best to orient them to efficiently serve the as yet imaginary population is all accounted for before any construction takes place. The designed city is carefully drafted along the lines of some mathematical system, dividing up parcels of land and connecting them to one another through a regular network of roads. It does not come into being organically as the result of reactionary responses to the meandering needs of the moment, as in the case of the first city, but is in every way intentional and deliberate.

Although both processes can result in a similar product—in this example, a city—the processes themselves are nearly antithetical, and we can see evidence of the differences between the processes in the form of the resulting cities, in spite of their being superficially alike.

Some might quibble about the differences here delineated between "design" and "organic creativity" on the basis that even the most meticulously planned project will include an element of unplanned or chance outcomes. Although things don't often go exactly according to plan, or maybe for that very reason, we cannot assume that any variation from a preconceived idea disqualifies a project from falling under the heading of "design."

Consider, for example, a carefully designed and drafted plan for decoratively tiling the floor of a building. If this plan were to be implemented, and the project completed, would we consider it a function of design only if everything were exactly in line with the preliminary drawings? Would the floor tiling cease to be the product of design were unforeseen variables to crop up in the process of creation? What if the designer had to make minor adjustments in the type or color of tiles used due to the unavailability of specific products? What if any element of the tiled floor were even millimeters out of sync with the original layout? Of course, in these instances, we would reasonably conclude that such variations do not disqualify a thing from being considered "design." There naturally has to be an allowance for some degree of unplanned phenomena within every function of design. Indeed, in many cases, creative individuals looking for a certain look, will deliberately build unpredictability and happenstance into the very processes they employ to make their work.

Think of the designers behind the punk album covers and posters of the 1970's and 1980's. A common technique that was used by these designers in order to create that raw, grungy look was to photocopy an image and then photocopy the photocopy again and again until the flaws and distortions that carry over from one copy to another multiplied, and the image became appropriately ragged and frayed. Using this process, there is no possible way to control or predict just where the imperfections, the grain, or the fragmentation will occur, but this does not undermine the intentionality of design. The "happy accidents" and the little moments of serendipity that appear in this kind of work as a consequence of the calculated unpredictability of the process are not as accidental as many would believe. Choosing to use difficult-to-control processes in the first place to capitalize on their intrinsic mark-making vocabulary is a design decision.

Even if it may be difficult to produce just the right mark, with this and other unpredictable processes, it is often not difficult to edit out or cover up marks that do not live up to the desired "look." By trial and error, keeping the desirable and discarding the undesirable, that which appears to be unpredictable or unplanned may ultimately be tightly controlled by the creator.

When so called "spontaneous" or "intuitive" techniques are used in a design capacity, they have no power to qualitatively transform a design function into a function of organic creativity. One might appropriate some of the qualities of organic creativity for use in a piece of design, but as the calculated use of unpredictable methods would constitute a design decision, we have to conclude that such a thing would still remain a function of design, which fact points us towards the most fundamental difference between design and organic creativity.

Perhaps the most obvious thing that separates design from organic creativity is intentionality; design is intentional, organic creativity is not. As soon as an individual determines to undertake the creation of something, they are already moving down the path of design. To say, "I will make. I will create. I will form." is in itself a plan. It is a manifestation of deliberate creativity, and is therefore within the province of design.

This is an important distinction to be made, as we discuss creativity, because it helps us to determine where art belongs in this discussion. Spontaneity, intuition, happenstance, instinct, and even occasional dumb luck are often valued highly by artists, but only insofar as these things can be utilized to serve a larger, deliberative vision. All art is intentional, not incidental, and therefore art does not happen by accident, even if artists are willing to exploit accidents. Art always arises as the result of a plan, and must therefore fall under the auspices of design.

Choosing to make art in the first place is a design decision. Deciding what scale the work of art will be is a design decision. Determining what materials, techniques and methods you will employ in the creation of that art is another design decision. Resolving what the work will ultimately look like in terms of color palette, subject matter, and composition is a design decision too. No matter how unpredictable, organic, or primitive a work of art may appear to be, it did not come into being without the artist first making some of these design decisions in advance.

These realities lead us to conclude that all art is necessarily a function of design, and this conclusion allows us to establish our second theory about things that are "not art."

"Anything that is not primarily a function of design is not art."

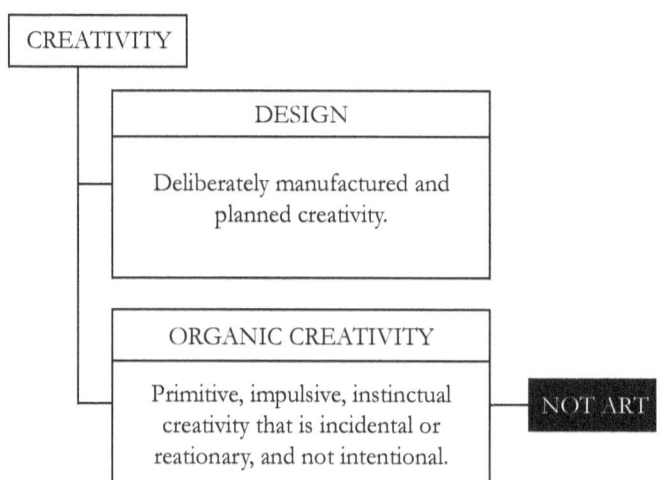

CHAPTER 7

Although all art is intentional, and is therefore a product of design, just because a thing is a product of design does not automatically qualify it as art. While all art might descend from design, art has a specific set of additional requirements not incumbent upon every other manifestation of design. Artist David Hockney wryly pointed to the distinction between art and design when he quipped, "Art has to move you and design does not, unless it is a good design for a bus."[43]

As evidence of this distinction, consider the following: a fitness trainer might carefully orchestrate a series of targeted exercises to help a client build strength in their core. Arranging the elements to be used in this exercise regime is a function of design, but it is not art. An educator who curates a set of materials, readings, assignments, videos, and assessments in the development of a curriculum is also involved in design, but not art.

Corporate strategists that engineer a merger or corporate takeover carefully plan for the most efficient and profitable disposition of the combined assets. This too, is a form of design, but it is not art. Each of these endeavors, while thoroughly subscribing to the requirements of design, are not art.

If not all of design is art then, within our taxonomy, "design" must be further subdivided. Four main categories can be formed as subdivisions of design, and they are as follows: *Product Design*, *Process Design*, *Organizational Design*, and *Ideological Design*.

Product design is principally concerned with the creation of things, such as cars, televisions, golf courses, fishing rods, packaging, clothing, buildings, and oil paintings. Product design is sometimes the means whereby things that have never before existed come into being, as with the invention of gunpowder, the printing press, the hot air balloon, and the camera. Sometimes product design is involved in the upgrade or modification of existing commodities, such as the advances made in everything from computers and machinery to construction and transportation. Product design is not strictly involved with the creation of just items, however. Among other things it also includes what could be better described as productions, such as performances, entertainments, and other gatherings or events.

Process design, on the other hand, is connected to the idea of procedure. As we have discussed, procedure revolves around following a set of instructions in order to arrive at a predictable solution to a given problem. The principle creation of such techniques, procedures, and formulas, however, are a function of design. Someone creatively formulates and records a sequence of steps to be followed in order to achieve a desired outcome, thus allowing someone to non-creatively accomplish the same task by following the recorded instructions. The creation of everything from surgical procedures to airline safety checks to legal proceedings is a function of process design.

Organizational design involves the manufacture of different kinds of collective relationships, ranging in scale from the family chore chart to the multinational industrial superpower. This kind of design arises from the need to tackle potentially complex problems. By subdividing a problem into a succession of smaller, more manageable tasks that are completed by a number of different individuals, an organization is able to accomplish wonderfully complex and difficult undertakings.

The formation of governmental, political, and civic entities such as nations, states, parties, militaries, legislatures, constabularies, councils, parliaments, and judiciaries all exist as a result of organizational design. This kind of design also serves business interests in the creation of companies, corporations, structured management, boards, supply chains, bureaucracies, and delivery systems. Every collective enterprise, from education and healthcare, to retail and finance, benefits from organizational design. The efficiency of each one of these collective concerns, no matter how large or small, is fundamentally connected to how well-designed the relationships are between all of the component parts.

Ideological design is the deliberately structured arrangement of concepts or ideas into a specific philosophy, code, or way of being. Philosophers, ethicists, and moralists are in the business of ideological design, as is every individual who considers what ideas they will support, and what kind of code they will allow to govern their lives.

We also frequently see this kind of design in institutions, businesses, and organizations. Huge state research universities and small liberal arts teaching colleges will invariably have different mission statements. Since they serve different populations, and their facilities allow for different kinds of educational experiences, they might embrace different philosophies about educational methods, and they may have very different ideas about what they want their students to get out of the experience that they provide. These philosophical differences are not accidental; they are a function of design.

Similarly, food companies that determine that their corporate philosophy will involve sourcing only organic foods; builders that will only use products or components made in the U.S.A.; and non-profit organizations targeting their services toward poor or underserved populations are all further manifestations of ideological design. In each of these scenarios, institutional leaders determine what they want the ideological focus of their concern to be, and they systematically design the organization to align with that core set of ideas.

Just about all endeavors in design can be collated into

at least one of these four categories, but not all outcomes stemming from these categories are art, even when employed by artists, or for the benefit of artistic endeavor. For example, artists have used ideological design to create manifestos and artistic doctrines, but no one (including the artists concerned) considers the formation of these ideas to be art. Artists have used organizational design to form workshops, guilds, groups, and schools, often with a complex hierarchical structure, but these organizations are also not considered to be a function of art. Artists have also developed myriad processes and techniques to be utilized in the creation of art, but while a process can *potentially* lead to the creation of art, the creation of the process itself cannot be considered as art. Because art is always a product, art is therefore only subject to the category of product design.

As we follow our taxonomy down through these tiers of categorization, we are able to add a third theory to our position about what is "not art."

"Anything that cannot primarily be considered a product is not art."

```
DESIGN
├── PRODUCT DESIGN
│   The deliberate creation of things,
│   items, objects, productions, events,
│   entertainments, etc.
│
├── PROCESS DESIGN                                  → NOT ART
│   The deliberate creation of formulas,
│   techniques, processes, procedures,
│   strategies, methodologies, etc.
│
├── ORGANIZATIONAL DESIGN                           → NOT ART
│   The deliberate creation and structur-
│   ing of collective relationships like
│   corporations, teams, governements,
│   institutional heirarchies, etc.
│
└── IDEOLOGICAL DESIGN                              → NOT ART
    The deliberate creation and arrange-
    ment of concepts or ideas into a
    codified philosophy or way of being.
```

CHAPTER 8

Since art has to be creative, a function of design, and ultimately a product or a production, there is a very real danger that we might start thinking that every creatively designed product is the same as art. It is not uncommon to hear people speak enthusiastically about sneakers as art, gardening as art, or cabinet making as art. Surely the creation of these things and others like them is a manifestation of creativity. We can furthermore admit that each of these things is also a function of design. What is more, they are all products. Without question, sneakers, gardens, and cabinetry meet the criteria of "product design," but we are not fully convinced that these things are art simply by meeting these criteria alone. If they are not art, then it must follow that we need to further partition the category of product design into additional subcategories.

In trying to understand whether or not a thing is art, it becomes imperative that we are able to draw conclusions about the ultimate function of that thing. On the nature and function of art, Oscar Wilde wrote, "We can forgive a man for making a useful thing as long as he does not admire it. The only excuse for making a useless thing is that one admires it intensely. All art is quite useless."[44]

It is important to make the distinction here that art being useless does not mean that it has no function. Wilde himself implicitly identifies the function that justifies the making of art, i.e. that it is something worth scrutinizing, studying, and admiring intensely.

If "useless" in this context does not mean "functionless," what exactly can it mean? Allow us to suggest that Oscar Wilde's employment of the word "useless" here describes something that is non-utilitarian, something whose function does not reflect a designated practical utility. For example, a clothespin has a very specific utility, and is therefore considered a utilitarian product. Claes Oldenburg's monumental *Clothespin Sculpture* does not have a specific utility, and is therefore a non-utilitarian product. A windmill also has a specific utility; a painting of a windmill, however, does not. A sweater has a utility; a poem about a sweater has no utility. A battery of cannons has a utility, but a martial composition for chamber musicians does not. Put simply, products that do not perform practical tasks are non-utilitarian.

Among those things that are a consequence of "product design," there is an important distinction to be made between things that are utilitarian in nature and things that are not. This distinction allows for a further subdivision of product design. For the purposes of our taxonomy, we will classify these separate areas as *Utilitarian Product Design* and *Non-utilitarian Product Design*. If all art is quite useless—or in other words non-utilitarian—we can identify, with a high degree of certainty, further things that do not belong in the conversation of art.

We recognize that the primary function of sneakers, gardens, and cabinets is utilitarian in nature. Though their creation is a function of design (like art is), and though they are each a product (just as art is), we are forced to conclude that if they are primarily utilitarian in nature, they cannot reasonably be looked upon as works of art. While we probably never really considered the design of sneakers as a serious art form, there are many things that we commonly seem to group together with art that, as fruits of utilitarian product design, end up falling under a different category from art.

For instance, many view the fields of industrial design, fashion design, and crafts as being closely related to, and perhaps indistinguishable from art. As these fields are responsible for shaping the look and functionality of everything from cars and microwave ovens to sweaters, socks, pottery, and textiles—all utilitarian products—their prime function is irreconcilable with the non-utility of art. All of these disciplines, and others with them, belong to a group within utilitarian product design that is principally concerned with the design of objects.

Architecture, interior design, and landscape design are further disciplines that are often seen as art. However, since these fields are concerned with the design of furnishings and lighting, gravel paths and espaliered fruit trees, malls and military bases—undertakings that are utility dominant—these fields are not to be confused with art. These, and other related endeavors belong to a group within utilitarian product design whose concern is the functional design of spaces.

Graphic design is another creative field that is frequently considered to be art. But since graphic designers deal with the design of utilitarian things like books, magazines, posters, packaging, and websites—each endeavor more utilitarian than the last—the focus of graphic design is materially bifurcated from that which brings art into being. Graphic design, data visualization, software design, propaganda and many, many other related enterprises find themselves as part of a group within utilitarian product design that is preoccupied with the design of information.

It may well be that directing stuff like fashion design, architecture, or crafts into the realms of "not art" is disagreeable to the sensibilities of some individuals. There may be those who protest that they have seen fabulously intricate and elegant examples of ceramics, blown glass, or even apparel presented as art in galleries and museums. If these works are the results of utilitarian product design, why would they possibly be presented in an unambiguously art context? Does not their presentation in this context suggest that they are art? And if they were to be considered art, would not their status as art undermine the stance that "all art is useless"?

When we go to a museum and we consider the massive, crusty, dinted, ceramic works of Peter Voulkos, or the scaled, cellular assemblages of Beate Kuhn, we are put to our paces to determine what, if any, reasonable utility these works could fulfill. Likewise, the viney glasswork of Lino Tagliapietra, or the fantastical, monstrous *Soundsuits* made by Nick Cave, defy any efforts to saddle them with some kind of distinguishable usefulness.

In the end, mediums are just mediums. Ceramics can be art and ceramics can be "not art." Glass can be art and glass can be "not art." So it is with apparel as well. Just because ceramics and glass, fashion and furniture design, architecture and textiles typically produce utilitarian objects does not mean that all the work made in these fields is automatically "not art." Art can come from all of these fields, but it can only do so once the work has ceased to be primarily utilitarian in function, or what we might term "utility dominant."

A thing's designation as "utility dominant" can be complicated sometimes. For example, a hammer is designed to drive nails, and insofar as it fills this function, it is utility dominant. But what happens when an old-fashioned hammer is hung on a wall as a decorative element? As a decoration, the hammer no longer serves any practical utility. Placing the hammer in this particular employment would be a transformative gesture, as, in the instant it is done, the hammer would shift from being utilitarian to non-utilitarian.

From this example, we come to realize that both

context and intention have a great deal to do with whether or not a thing should be labeled as utility dominant. The designer of the hammer intended the hammer for one thing, and the decorator intended the hammer for another thing altogether. What that hammer actually is—whether or not it can be considered utilitarian or non-utilitarian—is related more closely to the prevailing terms or context of its current existence than its initial intended function. In other words, when it was being used as a hammer, it was a hammer, but when it was reimagined as a decoration, it became a decoration.

Marcel Duchamp's *Fountain*—a readymade work consisting of a urinal signed by the artist—is a fine example of this phenomenon. In a literal, physical sense, there is no appreciable difference between the urinal one might find in a museum's bathroom and the *Fountain* one might find on display in a museum gallery. Both are made of the same materials, by the same process, and initially with the same end in mind. What principally separates them is this idea of intention.

By re-contextualizing the urinal from the bathroom to the gallery, Duchamp has intentionally reformatted how we look at the object. In so doing, he has taken something of utility, and has made it into an object of no practical use. As such, it is able to qualify as non-utilitarian, and is therefore conceivably capable of qualifying as a work of art as well.

The reverse can be true too. A printmaker might take stacks of old proofs and prints that are of no further use to him, mill them down into pulp, and with that pulp create sheets of handmade paper for editioning a new set of prints. This process would transform non-utilitarian prints into utilitarian paper, and by so doing would effectively convert something that might have, at one point, been considered art into something that would qualify as "not art."

As we can see, the utility or non-utility of a thing can be fluid. In spite of that, however, we needn't suppose that this ceaseless migrating back and forth between utilitarian and non-utilitarian function is the natural state of things. The examples we have cited are, if anything, outliers of the natural order. In most cases, a thing is created and designed with a specific function, and it retains that function to the very end of its days.

Because of this, we can confidently designate disciplines like industrial design, crafts, fashion design, architecture, graphic design, and many others as principally functions of utilitarian product design. We do so while being fully aware that occasionally these areas are made use of by artists, but since the overwhelming majority of what is made in these fields is made for purposes foreign to the enterprise of art, it is reasonable for them to be absorbed into the many categories of "not art."

In consequence of these determinations, we are able to establish our fourth theory about "not art."

"Anything that is primarily utilitarian in nature is not art."

```
PRODUCT DESIGN
    │
    ├── NON-UTILITARIAN
    │   PRODUCT DESIGN
    │   The design and creation of products
    │   and productions that have no practi-
    │   cal utility or survival value.
    │
    └── UTILITARIAN
        PRODUCT DESIGN
        The design and creation of products ── NOT ART
        and productions that have a practical
        utility and/or survival value.
```

CHAPTER 9

We have discussed a few of the areas that exist within the category of utilitarian product design, and we have argued a rationale for why these areas typically are not likely to result in the creation of art. We turn now to the examination of non-utilitarian product design to see if further categories can be delineated that will aid in the identification of "not art."

As already discussed, non-utilitarian product design can be recognized as the act of making things that have no practical utility. The more pragmatic among us might well ask, "Why would anyone take the time to deliberately create something with no practical usefulness?" This question seems particularly cogent when we consider how many practical labors we have to perform, and how many of those labors are in one way, shape, or form intrinsic to the simple realities of survival. We have already mentioned, however, that humankind has a penchant for impracticalities, regardless of the fact that we can easily recognize how little they contribute to our survival. Indeed, we as humans tend to spend vast amounts of our time engrossed in things not even closely related to survival—and we would likely spend more time doing so if we could.

Perhaps one reason for this proclivity is that we innately recognize that not all involvement in so-called "useless pursuits" is without profit. As Ovid wrote, "Nothing is more useful to man that those arts which have no utility."[45]

For the sake of clarity, Ovid's "arts which have no utility" refers to that collection of disciplines commonly known as "the fine arts," or even more simply as "the arts," which includes such things as literature, the performing arts, and the visual arts.

Ovid's discerning eye saw clearly that, as an example of non-utilitarian endeavor, the arts were at their roots impractical. However, he also asserted that, in spite of their non-utility, the usefulness of the arts was of paramount importance to mankind. The power that is in the arts to lift and inspire us, to shape our thoughts and dreams, and to help us to see with new eyes may not be practical, but in allowing us to momentarily shrug off the mean shroud of the daily round in order to witness a glimmer of truth, that influence becomes something of great worth.

To further allay any confusion, it is important to emphasize that the terms "art" and "the arts" are not intended to mean precisely the same thing, even though on the surface they would appear to be almost identical. It is tempting to conflate "art" with "the arts" as a way to streamline our path for understanding the former; but apart from the difficulties posed by making the statement "art is the arts"—including the inevitable posing of such questions as "What is literature?" or "What is music?" or "What is dance?"—simply stated, not every product stemming from "the arts" is very artful in nature. In order for us to better understand this distinction, we must further theorize about the different categories of non-utilitarian product design.

Non-utilitarian product design has seemingly been with us since the beginning. We find evidence of the arts even among prehistoric cultures, whose urgent preoccupation with survival presumably left them with little in the way of spare time. We are hard pressed to explain a cultural interest in non-utilitarian things, such as the arts, among peoples for whom utility would seem to have been everything. Again and again, however, the archaeological record reminds us that the arts form a thread that binds human society together all the way back to our principal ancestors.

Although, as far as we are aware, the design of non-utilitarian products has been a consistent aspect of human culture from the very beginning, the proliferation of different forms of this kind of design has naturally gone hand in hand with the advancement of civilization. As questions of survival diminished in urgency, so newfound disposable income and unencumbered time gave rise to a widespread preoccupation with finding some means of filling that time. In some cases, this meant expending time and effort in a search for some kind of meaning in existence—what we might call a search for truth—and in other cases, this entailed merely devising means for staving off boredom or existential dread. Under the heading of non-utilitarian product design, "decoration" and "entertainment" are two categories that are largely concerned with the latter interest.

Our modern usage of the word "decoration" stems from an early 15th century usage—*decoracioun*—that was used to describe "the covering of blemishes with cosmetics."[46] As this would seem to indicate, decoration is, at its root, more preoccupied with calculated deception than anything else. Decoration is primarily concerned with superficialities—i.e. changing the surface of a thing, and not its substance—and must therefore occupy its own space separate from art since, as discussed previously, art is concerned less with deception than it is with uncovering the truth.

Confusion about the relationship between art and decoration is common enough; indeed, many believe them to be one and the same. For instance, who has not heard these words uttered in reference to a beautiful painting, "That is the perfect size to hang over the love seat in the parlor" or, "Oh, those colors would really go well with the drapes in the guestroom" or, "It's lovely, but I'm only interested in pictures of cats." All of these statements, and others like them, are primarily focused on superficial attributes like size, color scheme, or subject matter—in other words, the concerns of a decorator—and fail to take into account the fundamental art of the thing. Confusing the decorative potentialities of art with its primary purpose for being reflects an odd infatuation with the art itself (i.e. the "lie" Picasso referred to, as discussed earlier) rather than the truth we are meant to realize *through* the art.

Many may find this distinction between art and decoration unsatisfactory. When we consider Michelangelo's Sistine Chapel frescoes, for instance, we may be tempted to point out their evidently decorative nature; and yet in spite of that apparent nature, these frescoes are widely viewed as being among the all time great masterpieces of art: a quintessential example of no-doubt-about-it art, if there ever were one. In this case, it might prove fruitful to compare Michelangelo's Sistine Chapel to examples of other, more obviously decorative pursuits, to see if we are able to distinguish an essential difference between them.

If we go back to Roman times, we are able to bear witness to a number of styles of wall painting, all of which were inescapably decorative in nature. Some wall paintings existed merely to create false illusions of a bigger space. Others were used to create false architectural adornments. Still others were employed to disguise the use of cheap materials by making them appear to be made of expensive marble. In a very real sense, these techniques were employed as means of covering the truth, rather than discovering it, which is antithetical to the aim of artistic endeavor.

If we were to fast-forward from Roman antiquity to the decorative programs of the French aristocracy in the 18th century, we would see more of this same kind of thing. During the Rococo era, the salons and palaces of the rich were routinely encrusted with carved plaster, gold leaf, painted motifs, ornaments, filigree, fluting, and every manner of decoration that could be devised by human ingenuity. The principal purpose of every one of these contrivances was solely an effort to dress up a space in an attempt to make it seem more significant, and by extension, to make the owner of the space appear to be of greater consequence as well.

Comparing the Sistine chapel with these primarily decorative undertakings, we find ourselves wavering in our stance that Michelangelo's work was only concerned with creating a facade, or a mere illusory manipulation. There is a clear difference between his work and the work of a decorator. For one thing, Michelangelo's work does not give the impression of greater significance, his work actually creates greater significance. Few people visit the Sistine Chapel for the sake of the space itself. Michelangelo's frescoes overawe their surroundings to the point that the original utility of the structure has almost become subsumed by the artwork. This has taken place to such a degree that we now generally consider the building's primary function to be that of housing and supporting the artwork. If anything, we see the chapel as a thing designed to enhance the frescoes, rather than the other way around.

Furthermore, Michelangelo's work is not mere vapid embellishment; it is packed with meaning, content, and purpose. His work is not about surface: it is about substance. At the outset of the project, Pope Julius II commissioned Michelangelo to "decorate" the ceiling, presumably because he had no notion of the difference between decoration and art. Michelangelo, who had no trouble in recognizing the difference between the two, refused Julius' commission, and instead worked up a completely different design that was to cover the ceiling with "art" instead of decoration.

Entertainment, like decoration, is also frequently seen as being connected with the arts. Plays, musicals, concerts, movies, television, comics, video games, pornography, and dime store novels are all widely considered to be products of the entertainment industry, and yet they appear to retain an ostensible connection to the arts because of their use of the arts' methods. However, like decoration, the purposes of entertainment are decidedly different from the purposes of art.

That which distinguishes the products of entertainment from those of art was stated succinctly by the poet W.H Auden: "[T]he only art today is 'highbrow.' What the mass media offers is not popular art, but entertainment which is intended to be consumed like food, forgotten, and replaced by a new dish."[47]

Because entertainments are designed to provide relief from familiar or mundane experiences, they must not themselves run the risk of becoming familiar. There is, therefore, a temporariness, a disposable "once and done" quality to things created for entertainment purposes. Syndicated comic strips that appear in newspapers everyday are a perfect testament to the limited shelf life of products designed to entertain. The comic is read, chuckled at, and promptly forgotten as the paper is discarded. There is no need to remember what was read, because a new set of comic strips will provide a ready chuckle with tomorrow's paper.

As alluded to above, entertainment is concerned with the creation of diversions and distractions that furnish opportunities to deliberately lose focus. Again and again, we see entertainment used as the recourse of those that no longer wish to think. People burdened by the anxieties of the day will deposit themselves on a couch and obliviate their cares by watching television or movies, playing video games, or surfing the Internet.

The philosopher and social critic Noam Chomsky put forward this observation on the diverting influence of certain media:

> [T]here are other media, too, their role is quite different: it's diversion ... The purpose of those media is just to dull people's brains; to get them to watch national football ... or get involved in astrology ... just get them away, get them away from things that matter. And for that it's important to reduce their capacity to think.[48]

This particular reality of entertainment is fundamentally different from the function of art. If art is to cultivate meaningful experiences, it has to demand of the viewer an even sharper focus; it *requires* them to think. Ultimately, entertainment differs from art in that it manufactures experiences that cause us to forget, whereas art is preoccupied with creating experiences that allow us to remember.

Some might argue that because they find viewing or experiencing art to be enjoyable, even entertaining, then all entertainment has the potential to be art. "What about a rock star?" they might ask. "Music is part of the arts, but in the case of the rock star, it can also be entertainment. Does that make the rock star an artist, an entertainer, or both?" When trying to make these kinds of assessments, what a thing is made for becomes more important than what a thing is made of, or how it is made. To determine whether or not a rock song, or a video game, or a work of pulp fiction is a function of the arts—let alone if it is art—or whether it is a function of entertainment, we need to take into account the main purpose or function of the thing itself.

In the case of the rock star question, we must ask ourselves, "Is the work of the rock star primarily intended for entertainment, or was it made for some other purpose?" If the answer is that the rock star's music is primarily intended for entertainment, then we must conclude that it cannot be art. We're not just picking on rock music here, or other popular musical genres; a great deal of classical music was also written for and used principally as entertainment. Insofar as an example of music, writing, painting, sculpture, dancing, acting, or any other thing is made with a dominant emphasis on entertainment, it consequently diminishes in its capacity to be art.

This is not to say that a work of art cannot be in some way entertaining, or even decorative. Clearly there is a certain quantity of overlap that exists between the arts, decoration, and entertainment. Things aren't always as neatly assigned to one of these categories as we might like. Obviously, some examples of art have decorative, and even entertaining aspects to them, but if those aspects are subsidiary to the overall purpose of the object—if the work is not entertainment or decoration dominant—than the object still has the potential to be art.

To highlight the importance of what a thing is made for in determining an object's dominant function—rather than what a thing is made of, or how it is made—consider the following examples.

Based on its dominant function, a painting of a cottage by John Constable can be a function of the arts. By the same token, a painting of a cottage by Thomas Kinkade's factory can be a function of decoration. Finally, a painting of a Thomas Kinkade cottage with a star destroyer flying through the misty morning light by Jeff Bennett can be a function of entertainment. As in all other cases, the best way to determine where an object fits in our taxonomy is to determine its primary—that is to say dominant—function.

For many, trying to tease out the difference between the three paintings listed above might seem like a pointless bit of pedantry. Indeed, some might argue that there appears to be no real difference between these images, either in medium or subject matter. But assertions like these ignore the significance of "why" a particular thing was made in favor of what a thing looks like. Artist Roy Adzak has said, "Good art is not what it looks like, but what it does to us."[49] What a thing does to us is intrinsic to why it was made, and why it was made determines where it belongs in our taxonomy of "not art."

We have indicated that while sometimes the products of both decoration and entertainment can superficially resemble the products of the arts, these areas of inquiry serve very different ends. Because of this, art can only possibly come from the arts, and this determination enables us to establish our fifth theory about those things that should not be considered art.

"Anything that is primarily a function of decoration or entertainment is not art."

```
┌─────────────────────────────────────────┐
│    NON-UTILITARIAN PRODUCT DESIGN       │
└──┬──────────────────────────────────────┘
   │   ┌──────────────────────────────────┐
   │   │            THE ARTS              │
   ├───┤──────────────────────────────────│
   │   │ The design and creation of       │
   │   │ products and productions within  │
   │   │ the realms of literature, the    │
   │   │ performing arts and the visual   │
   │   │ arts.                            │
   │   └──────────────────────────────────┘
   │   ┌──────────────────────────────────┐
   │   │           DECORATION             │
   ├───┤──────────────────────────────────│──── NOT ART
   │   │ The design and creation of       │
   │   │ products and productions         │
   │   │ primarily calculated to          │
   │   │ embellish, adorn, and give the   │
   │   │ illusion of magnified            │
   │   │ significance.                    │
   │   └──────────────────────────────────┘
   │   ┌──────────────────────────────────┐
   │   │          ENTERTAINMENT           │
   └───┤──────────────────────────────────│──── NOT ART
       │ The design and creation of       │
       │ products and productions         │
       │ primarily calculated to divert,  │
       │ amuse, and distract.             │
       └──────────────────────────────────┘
```

CHAPTER 10

Since each of the arts cultivates the soil from which art can spring, there are no further subdivisions that can be usefully made, and therefore it is with the arts that our formal taxonomy must conclude. However, while this taxonomy covers quite a lot of ground in helping describe what is not art, there still remain some important but informal distinctions to be made about "not art" that lie outside of the scope of this taxonomy.

For instance, while it is possible for art to be made in the fields of literature, music, theater, and dance, we typically call the work of musicians music, the work of playwrights theater, the work of dancers dance, and the work of authors literature. In like manner, we call the work of visual artists art. Most discussions about art, therefore, are chiefly concerned with visual art.

Additionally, when it comes to conversations about art, we have to observe that not all visual art is created equal. There is art, and then there is Art. Some art is good—even great—while other art is not. Good art and bad art all deserve to be considered art, but since bad art is generally not of particular interest, whenever we talk about art we are typically just talking about good art - Art with a capital A. By the same token, we only talk about music or dance or literature as art when they achieve this uppercase A status. We do not usually refer to vacuous novels, tedious choreographies, or insipid musical arrangements as art.

When we ask ourselves, "What is it that makes one work of art good and another bad?" we might initially wonder if there is any satisfactory answer. Upon mature consideration, however, we can at least conclude with a reasonable degree of certitude that since the function of art is to unearth some particle of truth, good art must be good in consequence of its revelatory capacity, and bad art must be bad, conversely, because of its failure to engender revelation.

This stratification between good art and bad art can lead some to protest. They might ask, "Isn't the determination of good and bad in art entirely subjective? Isn't art, like beauty, in the eye of the beholder? And isn't the success of a work of art subject to the tastes of individual viewers, and therefore relative?" It is common for people to suppose that all art is subjective, that everyone's opinion about a work of art is valid, and that there is no real right or wrong when it comes to art in general, but these suppositions are founded on the erroneous assumption that everyone has an equal stake or authority in determining the art question.

Imagine yourself in conversation at a social gathering when someone says, "Well, I may not know anything about theoretical physics, but I don't agree with Einstein. I just don't think that $E=MC^2$, so there." We might chuckle at the absurdity of such a remark, but we have to wonder, isn't this individual entitled to their own opinion? It must be admitted that yes, this person is allowed to have their own opinion on the subject, but since they know nothing whatsoever about theoretical physics, their opinion about mass-energy equivalency doesn't really matter much.

In the above example, while this hypothetical individual might be disqualified from having a meaningful opinion on physics because of his ignorance on the topic, does it follow that there is no one that could legitimately challenge Einstein on this issue? We would probably agree that Einstein could be legitimately challenged, but only by another similarly qualified theoretical physicist, or in other words, by another authority.

Extreme erudition, coupled with a wealth of specialized experience, places authorities much further up the mountain of truth than those not equally invested in a particular field of inquiry. As a result, authorities are able to survey a considerably wider horizon in their area of specialization than can the everyman. Because of this, we normally defer to authoritative positions on any given subject. For some reason, however, when it comes to art, not only do most people articulate very strong opinions about their personal likes and dislikes, but they will often do so in direct and deliberate opposition to established stances almost universally held by those with authority in art. Perhaps this is why Oscar Wilde quipped that, "Bad artists always admire each other's work. They call it being large-minded and free from prejudice. But a truly great artist cannot conceive of life being shown, or beauty fashioned, under any conditions other than those he has selected."[50]

We certainly recognize that everyone is free to have his or her own opinion, but everyone is not entitled to be right. The authorities in art can certainly be challenged, but it is implausible that any legitimate challenge would arise from a person lacking in substantial practical experience in the field of art. Simply put, in art, some opinions carry greater weight than others. This does not mean that everyone's taste will correlate with the authoritative, consensus view of art, but as taste has nothing to do with distinguishing quality, any dissonance between the tastes of the everyman and the positions of the authorities should not be considered particularly bothersome.

Some might wonder if there is any real value in our going to such lengths to deny so many enterprises the status of good art, or even simply art. Indeed, making the effort to deliberately deny art status to whole branches of human endeavor may seem to be exclusionary and elitist. After all, distinguishing a thing as "not art" could possibly be construed as a calculated effort to diminish the intrinsic worth of that thing.

It is easy to see why people might think this way, as the term art is frequently used in everyday idiom to denote a certain level of excellence. When we witness a particularly skilled dentist at work, we might say that he makes an art form out of drilling a tooth. When we see a seasoned professional install drywall rapidly and efficiently, we might, likewise, say that he is an artist. In our day-to-day experiences, we often think or speak of tasks that are well done as being "artful" and consider experts in every field as having made of their particular discipline an art. These vernacular connections between the term art and things worthy of admiration suggest a widespread cultural esteem for art and artists. Because of this cultural esteem, any suggestion that something is not capable of being art—in particular something that we admire—can feel a bit wounding.

Nevertheless, our purpose in distinguishing the difference between "art" and "not art" has nothing to do with building up the significance of the field of art at the cost of everything else. As was observed from the very outset of our argument, art is but one of many avenues that can be followed in the pursuit of truth. Just because a thing—or a whole industry or discipline—cannot be categorized as art, does not automatically diminish its usefulness as a conduit to truth.

If art is no better a method for discovering the truth than numerous other disciplines, what then is the use of art? For one thing, just because different items are of equal value, it does not follow that they are equivalent. Even if an apple and an orange were identical in their nutritional value, for instance, we would not imagine their flavor, texture, or scent—in short, their eating experience—to be likewise identical. So it is with art, as compared to other disciplines.

Returning to the analogy of the mountain, the vistas that open to our view as we climb the paths of art are unique; they are not available through any other avenue. Removing that spur of the mountain constituting art would materially diminish mankind's ability to achieve a comprehensive and well-rounded view of the truth.

It is for this very reason that forming a correct understanding of the difference between art and "not art" is important. If we wish to be acquainted with the truths that are specific to art, misapprehensions about what art actually is make it difficult—if not impossible—to know where on the mountain to make our ascent. To use another figure, it is like attempting to navigate a city while using the wrong map, or trying to bake a cake by following an automobile repair manual.

A car mechanic may bake a cake, if they choose, but they will find it difficult to do so unless they start in the right place, i.e. a cookbook. It is the same with art. Any genuine connection to the truths available through art must arise in consequence of understanding the realities that govern art.

This is not to say that the production of art is relegated to the few, or that none but professionals can contribute to the conversation. Nobel laureate T. S. Eliot, for example, was a banker by profession, and yet shook the literary world to its foundations in his spare time. Every lawyer, accountant, or insurance salesman whose professional pursuits do not qualify them as artists can, like T. S. Eliot, simply qualify as artists on their own time.

Since art is a discipline with specific limitations and requirements, the only thing preventing most people from being connected to art is an unwillingness to engage art on its own terms.

Art has to be creative and must be made deliberately, not incidentally. Art must also be non-utilitarian and cannot be a functionary of decoration or entertainment. Above all, art must bear witness of the truth.

These principles dismiss the confusing notion that art is everything, as well as the belief that art can be injured or diminished by prescribed boundaries. These principles also serve to upend the assumption that the field of art is without an authoritative consensus view. Gone is the supposition that art is the acme of human achievement; we understand instead that it is truth that forms the high ground to which all worthwhile human endeavor tends, including art.

Curiously enough, by simply seeking to understand what isn't art, we are able to see the question of art with new eyes. The clarity that comes with this understanding helps us to more perfectly orient ourselves towards what art is, and where we can go looking to find it.

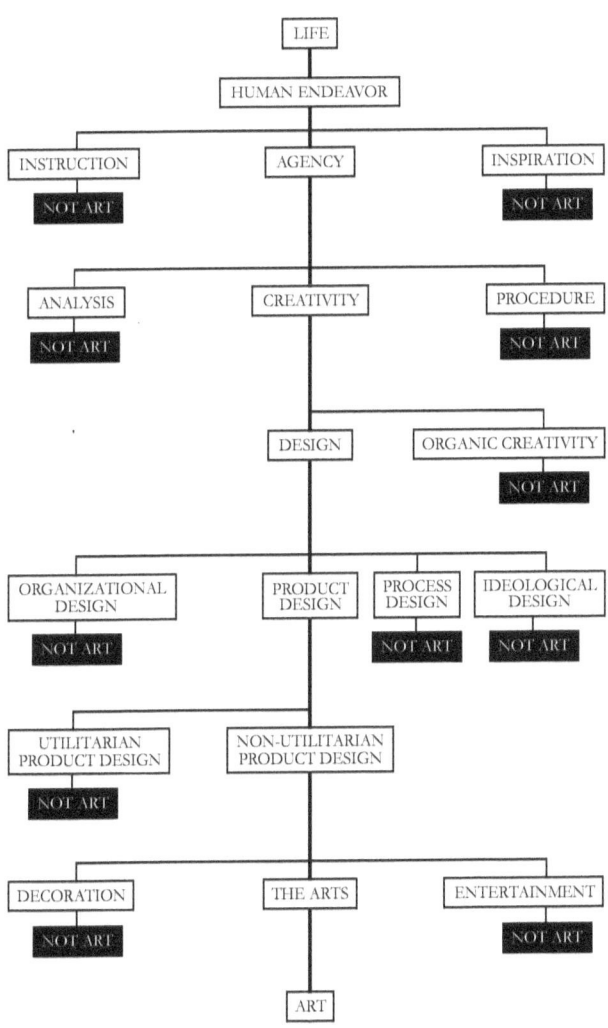

TAXONOMIC DIAGRAM

ABOUT THE AUTHORS

Ryan Muldowney is a native of Philadelphia, Pennsylvania. He graduated from the University of the Arts with a BFA in Illustration and from the Pennsylvania Academy of the Fine Arts with an MFA in Painting. His work is exhibited nationally and internationally in museums and galleries, and is represented in a variety of institutional collections. Mr. Muldowney has published numerous critical reviews and articles and is the author of eight books. Ryan Muldowney currently resides in Virginia and is an Associate Professor of Studio Art at Tidewater Community College.

Jacob Muldowney was born and raised in Philadelphia, Pennsylvania. He graduated from the Pennsylvania Academy of the Fine Arts with a BFA in Painting and from Washington University in St. Louis with an MFA in Visual Art. He maintains an active exhibition schedule and is the recipient of numerous awards and honors, including the Jason Penry Purchase Award, the Jack Kent Cooke Graduate Arts Award, the James P. Bonelli Jr. Memorial Prize, and the Lois and Charles X. Carlson Landscape Painting Residency. Jacob is currently an Assistant Professor of Art at Chowan University in North Carolina.

NOTES

[1] Galileo Galilei, *Dialogue Concerning the Two Chief World Systems—Ptolemaic & Copernican*, trans. Stillman Drake, 2nd ed. (Berkeley and Los Angeles: University of California Press, 1967), 225.

[2] Galileo Galilei, *Dialogues Concerning Two New Sciences*, trans. Henry Crew and Alfonso De Salvio (New York: Macmillan, 1914), 139.

[3] Tryon Edwards, *New Dictionary of Thoughts; a Cyclopedia of Quotations from the Best Authors of the World, Both Ancient and Modern, Alphabetically Arranged by Subject* (Charlotte, N.C.: Britkin, 1927), 663.

[4] Martin Adams, "Human Development From An Existential Phenomenological Perspective: 48 Some Thoughts And Considerations," *Existential Analysis* 24, no. 1 (January 2013): 49.

[5] Herbert Marcuse, *The Aesthetic Dimension: Toward a Critique of Marxist Aesthetics* (Boston: Beacon, 1978), 9.

⁶ George Sand, *The Haunted Pool*, trans. Frank Hunter Potter (New York: Dodd, Mead & Company, 1890), 15.

⁷ Clement Greenberg, "Modernist Painting," ed. Paul Wood, in *Art in Theory 1900-2000: An Anthology of Changing Ideas*, ed. Charles Harrison (Malden, MA: Blackwell, 2003), 775.

⁸ *Ibid.*

⁹ Vincent van Gogh. Vincent van Gogh to Theo van Gogh, July 21 1882. In *Van Gogh's Letters: Unabridged & Annotated,* translated by Mrs. Johanna van Gogh-Bonger, edited by Robert Harrison, number 218. http://webexhibits.org/vangogh/letter/11/218.htm.

¹⁰ Jacques Thuillier and Albert Chatelet, *French Painting: From Le Nain To Fragonard*, Early Edition ed. (New York: World Publishing Company, 1964), 252.

¹¹ Pierre Rosenberg, *Fragonard*, 1st ed. (New York: Harry N Abrams, 1988), 262.

¹² *Painters Painting,* dir. Emile De Antonio (United States: Arthouse Films and Curiously Bright, 1973), DVD.

¹³ Scott Edmiston, "New at CAMD: Professor of the Practice and Chair Scott Edmiston," Northeastern University College of Art, Media and Design, September 26, 2014, , accessed August 20, 2018, https://camd.northeastern.edu/2014/09/camd-professor-practice-chair-scott-edmiston/. par. 5.

[14] Ad Reinhardt, *Art as Art: The Selected Writings of Ad Reinhardt*, ed. Barbara Rose (Berkeley and Los Angeles: University of California Press, 1991), 53.

[15] Arthur Conan Doyle, *The Annotated Sherlock Holmes: Volumes I & II*, ed. W.S. Baring-Gould (New York: Clarkson N. Potter, 1967), 720.

[16] Elliot Murphy, *On the Mind and Freedom* (London: Lulu, 2011), 61.

[17] Bertrand Russell, *The Scientific Outlook* (Abingdon, UK: Routledge, 2001), 1.

[18] Paul Cezanne, *Letters*, ed. John Rewald (London: Bruno Cassirer, 1941), 234.

[19] Samuel Y Edgerton, *Pictures and Punishment: Art and Criminal Prosecution during the Florentine Renaissance* (Ithaca: Cornell University Press, 1985), 62.

[20] David Hume, *An Inquiry Concerning Human Understanding* (London: J.B. Bebbington, 1861), 5.

[21] John Chapman, comp., *The Westminster Review*, vol. XXXI (London: John Chapman, 1859), 33.

[22] Carolus Linnaeus, *Systema Naturae*, trans. M.S.J. Engel-Ledeboer and H. Engel (Nieuwkoop: De Graaf, 1964), 19.

[23] C.S. Lewis, *Mere Christianity*, First HarperCollins Hardcover ed. (New York: HarperOne, 2001), 226.

[24] Peter Schickele, *The Definitive Biography of P.D.Q. Bach, 1807-1742?* 1st ed. (New York: Random House, 1976), 2.

[25] *Gerhard Richter Painting*, dir. Corinna Belz, perf. Gerhard Richter (Germany: Zero One Film, 2011), DVD.

[26] Jennifer Trusted, *Beliefs and Biology: Theories of Life and Living* (Basingstoke: Pallgrave Macmillan, 2003), 84.

[27] Marjorie Grene and David Depew, *The Philosophy of Biology: An Episodic History* (Cambridge: Cambridge University Press, 2004), 77.

[28] Stephen Jay Gould, *Wonderful Life: The Burgess Shale and the Nature of History* (New York, New York: W.W. Norton & Company, 1989), 98.

[29] Richard Feynman, *The Character of Physical Law* (Cambridge, Massachusetts: M.I.T. Press, 1985), 34.

[30] Vimal Kishor, *Inspiring Thoughts of Great Educational Thinkers* (Pune, Maharashtra: Amitesh Publishers & Company, 2015), 118.

[31] Douglas J. Soccio, *Archetypes of Wisdom: An Introduction to Philosophy*, 5th ed. (Belmont, California: Thomson Wadsworth, 2004), 104.

[32] J. Harward, trans., *The Platonic Epistles* (New York, New York: Arno Press, 1976), 138.

[33] Arthur Schopenhauer, *Parerga and Paralipomena: Short Philosophical Essays*, trans. E.F.J. Payne, vol. Two (Oxford: Clarendon Press, 1974), §262.

[34] *Ibid*, §260.

[35] Richard Alan Krieger, *Civilization's Quotations: Life's Ideal* (New York: Algora Publishing, 2002), 184.

[36] C.S. Lewis, *The Four Loves*, (New York: Harcourt Brace Jovanovich, Inc., 1960), 103.

[37] Francis D. K. Ching, *Architecture: Form, Space, and Order* (Hoboken, New Jersey: John Wiley & Sons, 2007), ix.

[38] Joe Fig, *Inside the Painter's Studio* (New York: Princeton Architectural Press, 2009), 43.

[39] *Ibid.* 42-43.

[40] Frank Parkin, *Max Weber*, Revised ed. (London: Routledge, 2002), 34.

[41] "Andrew Wyeth Quotes," Andrew Wyeth: Biography, Paintings, Quotes, 2011, accessed September 18, 2018, http://www.andrewwyeth.org/andrew-wyeth-quotes.jsp.

[42] Joe Hefferon, *The Seventh Level: Designing Your Extraordinary Life* (Bloomington, Indiana: Balboa Press, 2012), 62-63.

[43] Tim Hilton, "Hockney Empire," *The Guardian* (London), October 26, 1988.

[44] Julian Wolfreys, ed., *Modern British and Irish Criticism and Theory: A Critical Guide* (Edinburgh: Edinburgh University Press, 2006), 20.

[45] Todd Bartel, "Jack Massey—Light & Dark," Thompson Gallery, December 2016, , accessed September 22, 2018, https://www.csw.org/page/news-detail-thompson-gallery-exhibitions-detail?pk=1073582#_ednref1.

[46] Douglas Harper, *Online Etymological Dictionary*, s.v. "Decoration," accessed September 19, 2018, https://www.etymonline.com/word/decoration.

[47] W. H. Auden, *The Dyer's Hand, and Other Essays* (New York: Vintage Books, 1968). 83.

[48] *Manufacturing Consent: Noam Chomsky and the Media*, dir. Mark Achbar and Peter Wintonick, perf. Noam Chomsky (United States: Zeitgeist Films, 2002), DVD.

[49] Ellen J. Langler, *On Becoming an Artist: Reinventing Yourself Through Mindful Creativity*, Trade Paperback ed. (New York: Ballentine Books, 2006), 58.

[50] Oscar Wilde, *Oscar Wilde's Wit and Wisdom: A Book of Quotations* (Mineola, New York: Dover Publications, 1998), 38.

BIBLIOGRAPHY

Adams, Martin. "Human Development From An Existential Phenomenological Perspective: Some Thoughts And Considerations." *Existential Analysis* 24, no. 1 (January 2013): 48-56.

"Andrew Wyeth Quotes." Andrew Wyeth: Biography, Paintings, Quotes. 2011. Accessed September 18, 2018. http://www.andrewwyeth.org/andrew-wyeth-quotes.jsp.

Bartel, Todd. "Jack Massey—Light & Dark." Thompson Gallery. December 2016. Accessed September 22, 2018. https://www.csw.org/page/news-detail-thompson-gallery-exhibitions-detail?pk=1073582#_ednref1.

Auden, W. H. *The Dyer's Hand, and Other Essays*. New York: Vintage Books, 1968.

Blumenau, Ralph. *Philosophy and Living*. Thorverton: Imprint Academic, 2003.

Cezanne, Paul. *Letters*. Edited by John Rewald. London: Bruno Cassirer, 1941.

Chapman, John, comp. *The Westminster Review*. Vol. XXXI. London: John Chapman, 1859.

Ching, Francis D. K. *Architecture: Form, Space, and Order*. Hoboken, New Jersey: John Wiley & Sons, 2007.

Doyle, Arthur Conan. *The Annotated Sherlock Holmes: Volumes I & II*. Edited by W.S. Baring-Gould. New York: Clarkson N. Potter, 1967.

Edgerton, Samuel Y. *Pictures and Punishment: Art and Criminal Prosecution during the Florentine Renaissance*. Ithaca: Cornell University Press, 1985.

Edmiston, Scott. "New at CAMD: Professor of the Practice and Chair Scott Edmiston." Northeastern University College of Art, Media and Design. September 26, 2014. Accessed August 20, 2018. https://camd.northeastern.edu/2014/09/camd-professor-practice-chair-scott-edmiston/.

Edwards, Tryon. *New Dictionary of Thoughts; a Cyclopedia of Quotations from the Best Authors of the World, Both Ancient and Modern, Alphabetically Arranged by Subject*. Charlotte, N.C.: Britkin, 1927.

Feynman, Richard. *The Character of Physical Law*. Cambridge, Massacgusetts: M.I.T. Press, 1985.

Fig, Joe. *Inside the Painter's Studio*. New York: Princeton Architectural Press, 2009.

Galilei, Galileo. *Dialogue Concerning the Two Chief World Systems—Ptolemaic & Copernican*. Translated by Stillman Drake. 2nd ed. Berkeley and Los Angeles: University of California Press, 1967.

Galilei, Galileo. *Dialogues Concerning Two New Sciences*. Translated by Henry Crew and Alfonso De Salvio. New York: Macmillan, 1914.

Gould, Stephen Jay. *Wonderful Life: The Burgess Shale and the Nature of History*. New York, New York: W.W. Norton & Company, 1989.

Greenberg, Clement. "Modernist Painting." In *Art in Theory 1900-2000: An Anthology of Changing Ideas*, edited by Charles Harrison and Paul Wood, 775. Malden, MA: Blackwell, 2003.

Grene, Marjorie, and David Depew. *The Philosophy of Biology: An Episodic History*. Cambridge: Cambridge University Press, 2004.

Harper, Douglas. *Online Etymological Dictionary*. Accessed September 19, 2018.
https://www.etymonline.com/word/decoration.

Harward, J., trans. *The Platonic Epistles*. New York, New York: Arno Press, 1976.

Hawking, Stephen, Nicolaus Copernicus, Galileo Galalei, Isaac Newton, and Albert Einstein. *On the Shoulders of Giants*. Philadelphia: Running Press, 2002.

Hefferon, Joe. *The Seventh Level: Designing Your Extraordinary Life*. Bloomington, Indiana: Balboa Press, 2012.

Hume, David. *An Inquiry Concerning Human Understanding*. London: J.B. Bebbington, 1861.

Kishor, Vimal. *Inspiring Thoughts of Great Educational Thinkers*. Pune, Maharashtra: Amitesh Publishers & Company, 2015.

Langler, Ellen J. *On Becoming an Artist: Reinventing Yourself Through Mindful Creativity*. Trade Paperback ed. New York: Ballentine Books, 2006.

Lewis, C.S. *Mere Christianity*. First HarperCollins Hardcover ed. New York: HarperOne, 2001.

Linnaeus, Carolus. *Systema Naturae*. Translated by M.S.J. Engel-Ledeboer and H. Engel. Nieuwkoop: De Graaf, 1964.

Manufacturing Consent: Noam Chomsky and the Media. Directed by Mark Achbar and Peter Wintonick. Performed by Noam Chomsky. United States: Zeitgeist Films, 2002. DVD.

Marcuse, Herbert. *The Aesthetic Dimension: Toward a Critique of Marxist Aesthetics*. Boston: Beacon, 1978.

Murphy, Elliot. *On the Mind and Freedom*. London: Lulu, 2011.

Parkin, Frank. *Max Weber*. Revised ed. London: Routledge, 2002.

Painters Painting. Directed by Emile De Antonio. United States: Arthouse Films and Curiously Bright Entertainment, 1973. DVD.

Reinhardt, Ad. *Art as Art: The Selected Writings of Ad Reinhardt*. Edited by Barbara Rose. Berkeley and Los Angeles: University of California Press, 1991.

Rosenberg, Pierre. *Fragonard*. 1st ed. New York: Harry N Abrams, 1988.

Russell, Bertrand. *The Scientific Outlook*. Abingdon, UK: Routledge, 2001.

Sand, George. *The Haunted Pool*. Translated by Frank Hunter Potter. New York: Dodd, Mead & Company. 1890.

Schickele, Peter. *The Definitive Biography of P.D.Q. Bach, 1807-1742?* 1st ed. New York: Random House, 1976.

Schopenhauer, Arthur. *Parerga and Paralipomena: Short*

Philosophical Essays. Translated by E.F.J. Payne. Vol. Two. Oxford: Clarendon Press, 1974.

Soccio, Douglas J. *Archetypes of Wisdom: An Introduction to Philosophy*. 5th ed. Belmont, California: Thomson Wadsworth, 2004.

Thuillier, Jacques, and Albert Chatelet. *French Painting: From Le Nain To Fragonard*. Early Edition ed. New York: World Publishing Company, 1964.

Trusted, Jennifer. *Beliefs and Biology: Theories of Life and Living*. Basingstoke: Pallgrave Macmillan, 2003.

Vincent van Gogh. Vincent van Gogh to Theo van Gogh, July 21 1882. In *Van Gogh's Letters: Unabridged & Annotated*, translated by Mrs. Johanna van Gogh-Bonger, edited by Robert Harrison, number 218. http://webexhibits.org/vangogh/letter/11/218.htm.

Wilde, Oscar. *Oscar Wilde's Wit and Wisdom: A Book of Quotations*. Mineola, New York: Dover Publications, 1998.

Wolfreys, Julian, ed. *Modern British and Irish Criticism and Theory: A Critical Guide*. Edinburgh: Edinburgh University Press, 2006.

www.ingramcontent.com/pod-product-compliance
Lightning Source LLC
Chambersburg PA
CBHW031426210526
45464CB00005B/2068